MOM'S
WODS

WORD OF THE DAY

DAILY DEVOTIONAL

MOM'S WODS

WORD OF THE DAY

DAILY DEVOTIONAL

BY
ELLA C. BRUNT

2015 first printing

Graphic Art Designer – Ben Williams
info@benwilliamsdesign.com

ISBN: 978-1-329-58379-5
E-Book ISBN: 978-1-329-62425-2

.

Printed in the United States of America

DEDICATION TO...

Our daughter Brittany who was the inspiration
for the concept, title and content
of this publication.

Our son Cody who shows his love and support
in such a kind and gentle way.

My loving husband Ted who is my technical
support system that kept me on track with
the layout and publishing tools.

To my long-time friend Bertie for her
editing expertise and suggestions.

My loving Heavenly Father Who gave His Word
in book form to supply the substance and
foundation of this book.

NOTES

In this manuscript numerous versions of scripture were referenced. The following is a key of abbreviations used:

AMP The Amplified Bible
GNB The Good News Bible
JNT The Jewish New Testament
JUB Jubilee Bible
KJV The King James Bible
MSG. The Message Bible
NASB The New American Standard Bible
NKJV The New King James Bible
NLV The New Living Version Bible
NTB Nave's Topical Bible
PHIL. The New Testament in Modern English by J. B. Phillips
TCNT The Twentieth Century New Testament
WMS The New Testament: A Translation in the Language of the People by Charles B. Williams

TABLE OF CONTENTS

ENDORSEMENTS

The best Acknowledgement I could ask for would be for the family and friends who have regularly received these Mom's WODS to write a note on how these thoughts have affected them. Thank you all for the encouragements along this journey.

****

Sometimes our souls need a little pick-me-up!

My friend Ella's inspiring and encouraging "mom's thoughts," are a great way to set our feet on a higher path and provide just enough Scripture caffeine to wake up our spirit.

This little treasure makes a lovely gift and a sneaky way to insert joy into the grumpiest of hearts. I love it!

- Reba Rambo-McGuire - singer, songwriter, musician

****

It was just a few months ago when Ella and I were sitting in my living room, lost in our thoughts and involved in our own early morning Bible studies. Reaching for my coffee, I took a moment to ponder the marvelous and amazing sister that was just a few feet from me.

"Lord Jesus! Thank You for the honor and privilege of knowing this daughter of Yours," was the initial thought in my heart. What consistency! What dedication! I had to admit I have known very few people who walk with God like Ella Brunt.

I have known Ella for 37 years. Has it really been that long? Having traveled together singing gospel music and ministering, and living through a multitude of different life circumstances together, I think I have seen Ella in just about every possible situation. In the midst of anything and everything, her walk with Jesus has always bannered two chief characteristics—Relationship and Faithfulness. If you are looking for religion, you will not find it here. If you are wanting a superficial, "feel good" insight into the ways of God, this is not the book for you. Ella will be quick to remind us all that it is the Truth of God's Word in a living relationship with Jesus that makes us free—nothing less, nothing more, and definitely nothing else.

In Mom's WODS, you have the opportunity to glean from Ella's amazing walk with the Lord what I have had the privilege of feeding from for many years—the pondering and musings of a heart that is totally yielded to Jesus. So, I invite you, the reader, to come and sit in the living room with my precious sister, and receive from the overflow of our Father's revelation in her heart.

- Bertie Jones Hall, MD & long-time friend

****

These daily devotions have provided encouragement to help start my day and have been a continuous reminder of how good God is. Whenever my mom started sending me her daily devotions I was going through a really tough time in my life. I was at the lowest point I had ever been. It truly felt like my life would never be the same, and that I would always feel alone. Having this daily devotion has helped open my eyes to all of the wonderful things that God has in store for my life. I have become aware that God has placed everyone on this earth for a purpose and that it is up to each one of us to fulfill it! I hope these devotionals encourage you the way they did me.

- Brittany Baye Brunt

****

Mom's WODs is an uplifting book that will give you a message of hope and encouragement every day of the year. For as long as I can remember, my mom has always been a constant and consistent cheerleader. She has supported me in absolutely everything I've ever attempted. I'm so thankful for that quality about her. My mom has always been someone I can trust. I can talk to her about anything! I have had the privilege of being exposed to and soaking up her wisdom my entire life. I know her book will richly bless you and give you a "word in season" just when you need it.

- Cody A. Brunt

****

Every day I look forward to receiving your Mom's WODS and as I read the Holy Spirit ministers to me... God is so good and totally utilizing your voice, "hearing heart" and ability to write to be the "vessel He is hosting"!!

So encouraged to know when it is God orchestrated, success is guaranteed!! You go Mom!

- Ginger Ramsey - fellow church member

Introduction

Motherhood was once only a dream that seemed unattainable in our marriage. BUT GOD came through and gave us two miracle children to complete us and bring us so much joy. Motherhood to young adult children gives way to a new dimension of watching them make their own paths and decisions. It's a process of knowing when to "let go" and give them the freedom to find their destiny, and yet still be there when "life situations" happen. I find I need to give them "space" to find their way as they learn to totally trust God to carry them through.

When we became aware our daughter was going through one of those "life situations," we prayed and trusted God. But knowing how powerful The Word is in any circumstance, I developed a "plan."

Each morning I would text Brittany a scripture and an encouraging/inspirational comment. I would time the "love text" when she was riding the bus to work to greet her each morning so she would know she was not alone and God would help her through. I would pray for the right scripture because I know the power of God's Word to change situations.

The texts were getting lengthy, so I started sending morning emails. I soon added Ted and Cody to the distribution list, then several young adults at our church, and later on friends and family members, so now it has evolved into a lengthy distribution list. The title of these love messages has changed from "Mom's Word of the Day" to "Mom's Thoughts" and finally to "Mom's WODS."

Now I enjoy exercise, playing tennis, yard work, etc. Brittany started doing CrossFit training early every morning before work. She invited me to join her on several Saturday workouts, which I did. This 62 year-old mom participated in the WOD (Work Out of the Day). I gained a great admiration for this extreme conditioning sport!

As I was preparing to publish the collection of these many "love texts," I changed the title of some of the older ones from Mom's Word of the Day to Mom's Thoughts. Brittany told me she had collected these in a folder labeled "Mom's WODS." She used this acronym **W**ord **O**f the **D**ay from her CrossFit daily WODS – <u>Workout</u> **O**f the **D**ay sessions. So as I began making final layout editing, we decided to change the title to *Mom's WODS*.

Due to copyrights, I was unable to use the word "CrossFit" in the title. Because of the scriptures used in this book, it is essential for you to know how The Cross <u>fits</u> in your life. Do you really understand the power of written Word of God? Do you realize the Bible is a collection of Love Letters to you directly from the Father God? Do you realize the power that is given to you to change situations? As you not only read The Word but when you speak and pray the Word, you have God's backing. So I'm not just giving my opinions in this manuscript, I'm using the Words of the Creator of the universe. HE is final authority in any situation.

The signature on my personal notes to Brittany has changed also, from "Love, Mom-Mom" to an endearing title some young ladies at our church have given me. They call Ted "Poppa Ted" and I am called "Momma Ella." So as the distribution list went from my immediate family, to many – this nick-name has been a treasure from them to me. I am privileged to have numerous "spiritual kids" that I have been their "cheerleader," encouraging them to go and do and be everything God desires for them to be.

Each daily entry is short and to the point. My desire and intent of publishing this devotional is to give you some "nugget" of wisdom, encouragement and inspiration that will carry you through the tough times, bring comfort in times of sadness, rejoice with you on the mountains and give hope in every situation.

Blessings always,
Momma Ella

JANUARY

1-1

REVELATION 21:5 KJV *"And he that sat upon the throne said, 'Behold, I make all things new'...."*

As we start a new year today, you have choices that you can make, adjustments to improve your life. When you trust Jesus totally, He can bring new things to you to bless you in ways only HE can. As this scripture declares, "He makes all things new". Trust Him to make this reality for you! HAPPY NEW YEAR!!!! ♡♥♡

1-2

2 CORINTHIANS 5:17 KJV *"Therefore if any man be in Christ, he is a new creature; old things are passed away; behold, all things are become new."*

There is no better place to be than "in Christ." As we live our lives in Him and for Him, there is peace, blessings, provisions, protection; every need is met in Him. ♡♥♡

1-3

ISAIAH 48:6 NKJV *"...I have made you hear new things from this time, even hidden things...."*

We need to have our attention on the things of God. HE is speaking and we need to be listening. Listening is an acquired skill. Lord, give us ears to hear and hearts to understand what YOU desire for us. We need to be Spirit-led and not head-led. ♡♥♡

1-4

ROMANS 12:12 NKJV *"Rejoicing in hope, patient in tribulation, continuing steadfastly in prayer;"*
Paul was writing in several verses (9-21) how Christians should behave. I picked this verse out because of these three things:
➢ We do have a hope that no other religious sect has
➢ The Love of God gives us patience to endure
➢ Most of all, as we continue to pray, we will be stable regardless of what we face. ♡♥♡

1-5

EXODUS 33:14 NLT *"The Lord replied, I will personally go with you, Moses, and I will give you rest—everything will be fine for you."*
Moses is talking with the Lord and was given this promise. I like to take it and receive it for me as well. We should desire to walk in His Presence all the time. There is rest, peace, and everything we need in His Presence. Always take time to be in His Presence – there is refreshing and peace that will strengthen you. ♡♥♡

1-6

EXODUS 33:15 NKJV *"Then he said to Him, 'If Your Presence does not go with us, do not bring us up from here'."*
Yesterday, we saw the importance of staying in His Presence. Moses knew this was so important that his response to the Lord was, "If you are NOT going on this trip with us, I'm not going!" Where God leads, He guides. Where He guides, He provides. Where He provides, He promotes. Where He promotes, He protects. Let Him take the lead of your life. ♡♥♡

1-7

ROMANS 12:17 KJV *"Recompense to no man evil for evil...."*

As we close this first week of January, let's make sure we don't carry any 'baggage' into this New Year. "Recompense" means to give back or pay back, to retaliate, to get even or to take revenge.

Rick Renner gives a good interpretation – "Don't get even with people by retaliating and taking revenge. You should never get into the business of intentionally trying to hurt someone just because they hurt you."

So, regarding the wrong things people have done to you – let them go. Whatever you do, get free from bitterness, anger, and strife. ♡♥♡

1-8

PROVERBS 3:9, 10 NKJV *"Honor the Lord with your possessions, And with the first fruits of all your increase; So your barns will be filled with plenty, and your vats will overflow with new wine."*

All of us want to prosper financially and this is the way you do it. Always give the Lord His portion and He will make sure ALL your needs are supplied. There are no shortcuts! Always give God His portion (10%) and He will make the 90% go farther than you could ever imagine. It's Kingdom living. ♡♥♡

1-9

JOHN 14:1 NKJV *"Let not your heart be troubled; you believe in God, believe also in Me."*

Most people in the world believe in a god of some kind. Jesus was telling the disciples, "Okay guys, you are good Jewish boys. You believe in God Jehovah...so believe Me too. There are benefits in believing...you don't need to be worried, fearful, or anxious about anything. I have your back. I can take care of everything you need and more." Trust HIM today for everything that concerns you. ♡♥♡

1-10

JOHN 15:16 NKJV *"You did not choose Me, but I chose you and appointed you that you should go and bear fruit, and that your fruit should remain...."*
What a precious declaration Jesus gave us. God Himself chose you and me. You are not an "accident" or "insignificant." He loves us and He needs us. We are to go and let the fruit that has been given to us bless others! Let our families, co-workers, neighbors, etc., see the goodness of God and desire what we have. Go bear some fruit today!! ♡♥♡

1-11

PROVERBS 3:6 NKJV *"In all your ways acknowledge Him, and He shall direct your paths."*
Are you building bridges, or are you building walls? As God directs (makes smooth or straight) our paths, plans, directions, decisions, etc., let them be bridges for you and others to cross over hard situations. He is The Way Maker! ♡♥♡

1-12

ROMANS 8:14 NKJV *"For as many as are led by the Spirit of God, these are the sons of God."*
When you make Jesus the Lord of your life, you enter into a new family. Not a physical family, but a Spiritual family, an eternal family of God. As a child of God, HE will make sure you are kept safe, provided for in every way – spirit, soul and body. Let Him lead you in paths of His righteousness. He desires the best for you! ♡♥♡

1-13

II TIMOTHY 3:1 NKJV *"But know this, that in the last days perilous times will come...."*

As we read in the Bible events that will be taking place in the "last days" before Jesus comes for us – we realize more than ever we are certainly in the last days. "Perilous" means something that is difficult, dangerous, or filled with risks. As Believers, we need to understand tough times are ahead of us, but God will always see us through and we will rise above the turmoil because we are "in Him." ♡♥♡

1-14

JOHN 16:18 NKJV *"They (the disciples) said, "What is this that He says, 'A little while'? We do not know what He is saying."*

Now the disciples were regular people just like us. Jesus was trying to let them know that He was going to be departing. They didn't understand everything Jesus taught the first time they heard it. So as we study His Word – ask Him to show you what He is saying. The Holy Spirit lives in you and will clarify His Word. Seek Him and He will give us understanding. ASK. ♡♥♡

1-15

PROVERBS 10:11 NKJV *"The mouth of the righteous is a well of life."*

It is so very important to watch what we speak from our mouths. Our words carry a creative force. We are the righteousness of Christ. We have His righteousness. So let our mouths _speak_ His righteousness. Our words will bring peace, healing, and kindness. Your words are powerful. Make them count. ♡♥♡

1-16

JOHN 17:3 NLT *"And this is the way to have eternal life - to know You, the only true God, and Jesus Christ, the One You sent to earth."*

Jesus was in the garden praying for us!!! He was asking His Father for us to know God as Father, the only true God, and to know Jesus. Years ago, Jesus was praying for us and still is today.

(Continued on the next page)

(Continued from previous page)
 He IS our Intercessor. He asks the Father for us and we can know Jesus, and we can know God as Father. This IS eternal life because our eternity WITH HIM begins when we make Jesus Lord of our lives. There is no time-limit on prayer and prayers are heard by your Heavenly Father. You are loved! ♡♥♡

1-17

PSALM 37:7 NKJV *"Rest in the Lord, and wait patiently for Him;"*
When we have prayed and asked the Lord for things, between the asking and the manifestation there is a waiting period. We are to rest in the Lord – know that He heard our prayer, then wait patiently. Another definition for 'patience' is cheerful endurance. While you are waiting on the Lord, rest in Him and remain patient. ♡♥♡

1-18

PSALM 37:37 NKJV *"Mark the blameless man, and observe the upright; for the future of that man is peace."*
Often times, children are asked who their "hero" is. As adults, we have our 'heroes' we look up to – people with Godly character, wholesome people, etc. As we continue observing these 'hero' people, God's Word instructs us to "mark them," pay attention to the way they live and see how they live in peace. Godly character opens the door to live in peace. ♡♥♡

1-19

PROVERBS 4:5 NKJV *"Get wisdom! Get understanding! Do not forget, nor turn away from the words of My mouth."*
The understood subject here is 'you.' You have a part to play to get wisdom and understanding – it doesn't just happen. The scripture instructs you to get wisdom and you to get understanding. The only source of those two benefits is God's Word. The time you spend reading the Word is never wasted time. The Word gets inside you and changes you. Let it be a daily practice to read His Word and let the Word build you up in wisdom and understanding.
(Continued on the next page)

(Continued from previous page)
There are two master teachers in life...wisdom and consequences. We get to choose which one we follow. Your choices matter. WISDOM - GO GET IT!!! UNDERSTANDING – GO GET IT!! ♡♥♡

1-20

ECCLESIASTES 8:12B NKJV *"...yet I surely know that it will be well with those who fear God, who fear before Him."*
As we honor (fear) God in the way we speak, the way we live, the way we obey His Word – He will make sure things will go well for us. As we honor Him, He will honor us. ♡♥♡

1-21

EZEKIEL 34:26 AMP *"And I will make them and the places round about My hill a blessing, and I will cause the showers to come down in their season; there shall be showers of blessing [of good insured by God's favor]."*
God desires to 'show out' through you!!! HE desires to bless you—HIS favor is on you. There are seasons in your life; there is a place He sets you in; and HE promises there He will shower His blessings on you! ♡♥♡

1-22

EZEKIEL 34:27B AMP *"And [My people] shall be secure in their land, and they shall be confident and know (understand and realize) that I am the Lord."*
The news daily shows terrors and calamities. As Believers, God has promised our safety regardless of what is happening around us. You will be kept safe and you will know that Jesus IS the Lord keeping your life safely in His hands. ♡♥♡

1-23

EZEKIEL 34:31 AMP *"And that you are My sheep, the sheep of My pasture;"*
Jesus is the Good Shepherd. We also see that in Psalm 23 and in John 10:11. A sheep is very dependent on its shepherd. Jesus likens us to a sheep for a reason. Stop trying to MAKE things happen – rather, trust Jesus with your life and HE will provide everything you need, exactly when you need it. [If you make it happen by your own effort – you have to maintain it. When you let God make it happen - He will maintain it.] ♡♥♡

1-24

PROVERBS 3:24 NKJV *"When you lie down, you will not be afraid; Yes, you will lie down and your sleep will be sweet."*
Sleep is necessary to refresh, strengthen and heal our body. Without enough sleep, we cannot think properly and every area of our mental and physical body is affected. If you have a hard time falling asleep – claim this scripture. Say it out loud. God's promise to you is to live full of peace and enjoy sweet sleep! ♡♥♡

1-25

PSALM 16:1 NKJV *"Preserve me, O God, for in You I put my trust."*
T-r-u-s-t is a very big word and an even bigger action to perform. IF you really trust someone, you are "all in." Your confidence and your total dependence are given to them. When you trust someone, you are in a vulnerable position – but In Jesus, HE will never exploit our trust. He will preserve, protect and provide your every need. ♡♥♡

1-26

JOEL 2:32 NKJV *"And it shall come to pass that whoever calls on the name of the Lord shall be saved."*
Joel was looking TO the time when Jesus would come and make the WAY for us to call on His Name to be saved. NOW is that time Joel looked forward to! We not only call on His Name for salvation, but also safety, protection, provisions, everything we need. ♡♥♡

1-27

LUKE 2:40 NKJV *"And the Child grew and became strong in spirit, filled with wisdom; and the grace of God was upon Him."*
Jesus was born and grew physically, mentally and spiritually – just like us. You have the capacity to grow and become spiritually strong as you study His Word. Gain wisdom (proper application of knowledge) and God's favor will be on you!!! ♡♥♡

1-28

MATTHEW 17:27B NKJV *"...you will find a piece of money; take that and give it to them (the tax collectors) for Me and you."*
It will soon be tax time. Jesus not only paid His taxes but in this verse, paid for Peter's as well. We are to be good citizens and pay the taxes we owe. Be honest and pay what your obligation. You may need to believe God for the extra money, but He will provide!!! ♡♥♡

1-29

I CORINTHIANS 15:17 NKJV *"And if Christ is not risen, your faith is futile; you are still in your sins!"*
Intellectuals have a hard time believing spiritual things. This scripture is bedrock to Christianity. Jesus came to carry all our sin, pay the price for our redemption and make the way for us to be righteous in His righteousness. It doesn't make sense to our senses - it is spiritually understood by faith. Thank God His Word is Truth, you can receive it by faith, and KNOW He is God and we are His children. We are forgiven of all our sins and Christ is risen indeed!!! ♡♥♡

1-30

EPHESIANS 5:1 NLT *"Imitate God, therefore, in everything you do, because you are His dear children."*
We have all seen little children imitate their parents. They act out something they have seen their parents do. Paul encourages us to imitate our Father God in character, actions and speech. Get so close to Jesus that people recognize His life being fulfilled in you. ♡♥♡

1-31

PHILIPPIANS 1:27 AMP *"Only be sure as citizens so to conduct yourselves [that] your manner of life [will be] worthy of the good news (the Gospel) of Christ...."*
The saying "Your life may be the only Bible some people read" is so true. Paul is encouraging Believers to live their lives as Godly examples as good citizens of this world and the Gospel. People are watching the way you conduct your lives and conversations – be a good reflection of Jesus!!! ♡♥♡

FEBRUARY

2-1

ROMANS 7:18 KJV *"For I know that in me (that is, in my flesh) dwelleth no good thing...."*
In our humanity, compared to God's glory, we have to admit that in our flesh we are not capable of doing "good." BUT when we allow God's ability to work in our humanity, we can accomplish His good pleasure. Be available to Jesus today – HE needs you! ♡♥♡

2-2

PSALM 18:19 KJV *"He (God) also brought me out into a large place; He delivered me, because He delighted in me."*
Whatever you may be going through right now – God can and will bring you through it. He is going through it with you because God loves you and delights to have you as His child. ♡♥♡

2-3

ROMANS 8:31B KJV *"...If God be for us, who can be against us?"*
Think about it! God, the creator of the universe, is your heavenly Father. There is nothing that can come against you that God cannot rescue you out of. You have to settle the "if." You have to <u>know</u> that God is for you, God loves you and God will help you. ♡♥♡

2-4

PSALM 20:4 NKJV *"May HE grant you according to your heart's desire, and fulfill all your purpose."*
My prayer for you today is that God will give you the desires of your heart and you will fulfill everything HE has purposed for you to do. You are here for a purpose and HE will equip you to make sure you accomplish His purpose in you. ♡♥♡

2-5

I THESSALONIANS 5:16 NKJV *"Rejoice always."*
This two word verse is harder to do that it seems. This is <u>not</u> a suggestion. This is <u>not</u> something you do if you feel like it. Things will come to take the joy out of your life. You have to make the decision in your heart to rejoice on purpose. 'To rejoice' - is a powerful force that empowers you to overcome in the hardest times. ♡♥♡

2-6

PSALM 27:1B NLT *"The Lord is my fortress, protecting me from danger, so why should I tremble?"*
When we are "in Christ", we are in good hands and much better than All State Insurance! HE is our protection from the deception in this world. As terror grows and the world systems fail, we don't have anything to fear. We trust in Him and HE will always hold us tight! ♡♥♡

2-7

2 PETER 3:18A NKJV *"but grow in grace and knowledge of our Lord and Savior Jesus Christ."*
Grow up! There is always more to know, more places in our lives to improve. As individuals we are all life-long-learners. We never reach a level that we have learned everything. Peter encourages us "to grow." That means we have to put forth the effort to read the Word, listen to teaching CDs, etc. You MUST make time and on purpose we seek the things of God. As you do, you will 'grow' in grace and knowledge. Seek Him, seek His grace and His knowledge. He desires to see you grow more than you realize. You and Jesus are a team!! A winning team!!! ♡♥♡

2-8

I JOHN 5:14 NKJV *"Now this is the confidence that we have in Him, that if we ask anything according to His will, He hears us."*
Sometimes we think (feel) God may not hear our prayers. This verse lets us know what kind of prayers God hears – prayers we pray according to His Will – which is His Word!!! Find a scripture that concerns your desire and pray it to God. We have confidence that He hears prayers in line with His will. HIS Will <u>is</u> His Word. ♡♥♡

2-9

ZECHARIAH 13:9B NKJV *"They will call on My name, and I will answer them. I will say, 'This is My people'; And each one will say, 'The Lord is my God'."*
It is so reassuring that WHEN we call – HE promises to answer us. As we call Him Lord, He calls us His people. What a great group to be a part of!!! ♡♥♡

2-10

ISAIAH 33:6 NKJV *"Wisdom and knowledge will be the stability of your times, and the strength of salvation; The fear of the Lord is His treasure."*
Knowledge is the intake of God's Word. Wisdom is the correct application or output of that knowledge of God's Word. In these last days before Jesus comes, it will get darker and worse, but God in us will shine brighter and brighter. His Word will be our "stabilizer" to keep us strong and full of peace. As we reverence and give God first place in our lives, He will be able to give us His wisdom, His knowledge and stability. Nothing else can do that. Only God can give us stability and a confidence that will be our strength to go through anything and come out victorious! ♡♥♡

2-11

EXODUS 19:5 AMP *"Now therefore, if you will obey My voice in truth and keep My covenant, then you shall be My own peculiar possession and treasure from among and above all peoples; for all the earth is Mine."*

God was training the Israelites in the wilderness. After 40 years, you might say they were "slow learners." It proves that just because you actually see miracles, you have to use your faith to believe God is God. God IS in charge and He desires our obedience to listen and obey His voice. He is speaking today – are you listening? ♡♥♡

2-12

EXODUS 19:4B MSG. *"…and how I carried you on eagles' wings and brought you to Myself."*

What a picture!!! Even though the Israelites were in the wilderness, HE literally carried them through. He delivered bread in the morning and quail in the evening and a huge rock "followed them" that provided water. If He did that for those "disobedient sheep" – just think how He wants to take care of your every need. ♡♥♡

2-13

MATTHEW 23:8B NLT *"…all of you are equal brothers and sisters."*

If you have been associated with a "church" for any length of time – they call each other brother_____ and sister _____ for this reason. We are members of the family of God. Members of the church are our brothers and sisters in the Lord. What a BIG family we have, but each one of us has our part to add to the church and fulfill what God has us here on earth to do. You have much worth and value!!! ♡♥♡

2-14

PSALM 27:10B NLT *"...the Lord will hold me close."*
This is Valentine's Day, so I am sending you a BIG HUG!!!!
Whatever you are facing – the Lord will hold you close and watch over you. Spend some time with HIM today. Allow the arms of God to envelope you with His love!!!!! ♡♥♡

2-15

PSALM 27:13 NLT *"Yet I am confident I will see the Lord's goodness while I am here in the land of the living."*
We don't have to wait until we get to heaven to enjoy God's blessings. We can enjoy the good things from God right here and now. We are a blessed people, His beloved! What an endearing name to call us. Be confident that God is good and HE really does LOVE you!!! ♡♥♡

2-16

I CORINTHIANS 1:4 NKJV *"I thank my God always concerning you for the grace of God which was given to you by Christ Jesus."*
I agree with Paul – I get excited to see how the Lord is blessing you, daily giving you HIS grace and mercy. I thank God for you today. Have a thankful heart for all God's gifts. ♥ ♡

2-17

PSALM 32:1 NLT *"Oh the joy for those whose disobedience is forgiven."*
Every day we should thank Jesus for the enormous price He paid so we can have forgiveness of our sins and shortcomings. That is enough to put joy in our hearts. ♡♥♡

2-18

ISAIAH 28:11 NKJV *"For with stammering lips and another tongue He will speak to this people."*

(*For the remainder of the month, we will look at the power of the Holy Spirit. If the Word says it – I believe it.)

I always like to have several scripture verses when I study doctrines in the Bible. Isaiah mentions the time period when the Lord will speak to His people as we seek Him and pray in the Spirit. This "inside information track" can be yours as you allow His Spirit to pray through you. His message goes past your head right into your spirit – spirit to spirit. ♡♥♡

2-19

JOHN 14:16 NKJV *"And I will pray the Father, and HE will give you another Comforter...."*

Jesus' last lesson to His disciples was that even though He was leaving, they would have ANOTHER come to be with them. ANOTHER is the Greek word "*allos*". This means one of the very same kind, same character; same everything; or a duplicate. Wow - the Holy Spirit is all that to us! We are NEVER alone; the Greater One lives in us!!!! ♡♥♡

2-20

JOHN 15:26A AMP *"But when the Comforter (Counselor, Helper, Advocate, Intercessor, Strengthener, Standby) comes...."*

Jesus promised when He left, God would send the Holy Spirit to be all these helps to us. Whatever you are going through, the Holy Spirit indwells you to equip you to overcome. ♡♥♡

Ella C. Brunt

2-21

ZECHARIAH 4:6B NKJV *"Not by might nor by power, but by <u>My Spirit</u> says the Lord of hosts."*
We are spiritual beings, made in the image of God. In this verse, even God did not depend on His might or His power to get things done. By His example, always rely on His Spirit within you to see God's Will accomplished in your life. Be Spirit-dependent. ♡♥♡

2-22

ACTS 19:2 NKJV *"Did you receive the <u>Holy Spirit</u> when you believed?"*
Paul's ministry was to the Gentiles. He took The Gospel to the Gentile nations; non-Jews. In Ephesus, he found several Believers and asked them this question. Paul made sure they not only believed in Jesus for salvation, but told them there was more. How do you answer this question? ♡♥♡

2-23

ACTS 1:4B AMP *"…He commanded them not to leave Jerusalem but wait for what the Father had promised…."*
This is Jesus' last instruction during the last 40 days after His resurrection. Jesus didn't make this a 'suggestion.' He commanded them. Take advantage of everything God has given you in His Word. ♡♥♡

2-24

ACTS 1:5 NLT *"John baptized with water, but in just a few days you will be baptized with the <u>Holy Spirit</u>."*
There is a physical baptism we participate in to show our death and resurrection life in Jesus. This is a spiritual baptism of Holy Spirit empowerment! Jesus was leaving, but He was letting us know God was going to fill in the gap to join us to Himself. What a plan! ♡♥♡

2-25

ACTS 1:8 NKJV *"But you shall receive power when the <u>Holy Spirit</u> has come upon you; and you shall be witnesses to Me...."*
Luke is quoting Jesus' instructions just before He departed. Jesus was about to go back to heaven, but He was not going to leave us comfortless and powerless. The Comforter has been given to us, to abide in us, to empower us! ♡♥♡

2-26

ACTS 2:4 AMP *"And they were all filled (diffused throughout their souls) with the <u>Holy Spirit</u> and began to speak in other (different, foreign) languages (tongues), as the Spirit kept giving them clear and loud expression [in each tongue in appropriate words]."*
In the Upper Room gathering, 120 met in unity and received the Holy Spirit with the evidence of speaking in languages they never learned. The prophecy Jesus gave them became a reality. They were ALL filled. This outward manifestation of the Spirit continues today to give Believers the fullness of His Presence. ♡♥♡

2-27

ACTS 19:6 NLT *"Then when Paul laid his hands on them, the <u>Holy Spirit</u> came on them, and they spoke in other tongues and prophesied."*
Hopefully you can read the entire 19th chapter of Acts to get the full picture of what is going on with Paul. Yes, as Believers in Jesus, salvation is ours and heaven is our home, but there is more to receive if you desire ALL God has provided for you. Be willing to receive everything God desires to give you. ♡♥♡

2-28

I CORINTHIANS 14:22 AMP *"Thus [unknown] tongues are meant for a [supernatural] sign, not for believers but for unbelievers [on a point of believing]...."*

This whole chapter 14 deals with speaking in tongues by the Holy Spirit. Believers understand the realness of this practice of praying in the Spirit. Unbelievers recognize this as a supernatural gift from God. On the Day of Pentecost (50 days after Jesus was raised from the dead) the citizens of Jerusalem heard those 120 Believers speak in tongues (unlearned languages) and it was a sign they had been with the Lord. Tongues are for today to build you up. ♡♥♡

2-29 (LEAP YEAR)

ESTHER 9:12 NLT *"But now what more do you want? It will be granted to you, tell me and I will do it."*

Talk about "favor" with the king.... Esther risked her life to approach the king without an invitation. The king's right-hand man had a plot to destroy the Jewish population. After Esther intervened and told the king what was happening and asked him to stop it, the king helped her. When things were settled, the king again asked her what he could give her. Today we have the favor of God on our lives also, and Jesus is the King of Kings!!! Can you envision your Father God asking you "But now what more do you want?" Wow – what a question, but you have to ask. ASK and you will receive! ♡♥♡

MARCH

3-1

PSALM 32:5C NLT *"You forgave me! All my guilt is gone."*
God's forgiveness is mentioned so many times in The Word. God
wants us to make sure we understand that in His forgiveness there is
<u>NO</u> <u>GUILT</u>. You are forgiven now so let it go!!!!! Be guilt-free! ♡♥♡

3-2

PSALM 33:4 NLT *"For the word of the Lord holds true, and we can
<u>trust</u> everything He does."*
"Trust" is such a small word to mean so much. Do you really totally
trust the Lord? Can you release your family and yourself to His care
unconditionally? This verse lets you know that God's Word IS truth.
When you find a promise in His Word you can trust Him to do it.
♡♥♡

3-3

LAMENTATIONS 3:22B, 23 KJV *"...because His compassions fail not.
They are new every morning: great is thy faithfulness."*
The Lord is moved with compassion when we 'hit the wall' in life. It
is not just a 'feeling' that He has for us, He is driven to act and reach
out to you. You can count on Him – He IS Faithful! HE is there for
you every day of your life. ♡♥♡

3-4

HEBREWS 4:9 NKJV *"There remains therefore a rest for the people of
God."*
Are you tired? God promises a rest for you. There is nothing like
being in a place of 'rest' from laboring so hard to make things
happen. As we trust the Lord with everything, we can enter into the
peace and rest only He can give. ♡♥♡

3-5

JAMES 1:22 KJV *"But be ye doers of the word, and not hearers only, deceiving your own selves."*
Intake of God's Word is what James calls being *'hearers* of the Word.' Putting out the Word is being a *'doer* of the Word.' Getting knowledge takes discipline to take the time to study the Word. As you gain knowledge, you can ask God to give you wisdom to apply it correctly. The last part of the verse lets us know deception is a possibility if we only hear it and don't do the Word. ♡♥♡

3-6

II TIMOTHY 2:15 KJV *"Study to show thyself approved unto God, a workman that needeth not be ashamed, rightly dividing the word of truth."*
God's Word is TRUTH. The Bible is still the #1 bestselling book of all time! Every time you read it, this Word is alive and fresh. God reveals Himself to you. God wants to talk to you through His Word. "Rightly dividing the word of truth" is wisdom – the correct application of knowledge. Never get bored by reading His truth to you.♡♥♡

3-7

JAMES 1:5 NKJV *"If any of you lacks wisdom, let him ask of God...."*
We have been discussing knowledge and wisdom the past few days, so this scripture guarantees us the ability to receive wisdom. As you study His Word, THEN, He can reveal to you His wisdom. God can and will open our hearts and minds to receive wisdom. ♡♥♡

3-8

*For the next week, let's take a closer look at the Beatitudes
Beatitude #1
MATTHEW 5:3 NKJV *"Blessed are the poor in spirit, for theirs is the kingdom of heaven."*
(Continued on the next page)

(Continued from previous page)

The Greek word for 'blessed' is *makarios* which means "happy, jubilant." 'Poor' means 'to be destitute or bankrupt.' We will see how the Beatitudes are progressive – from young and immature to maturity; from taking in to giving out. In this verse, spiritually we were empty when we accepted Jesus as Lord (the spiritual new birth). We didn't stay that way because Jesus gave us everything in the Kingdom of heaven!! ♡♥♡

3-9

Beatitude #2

MATTHEW 5:4 NKJV *"Blessed are they that mourn, for they shall be comforted."*

Salvation doesn't exempt you from difficulties – but you are NEVER alone, The Comforter (John 14:16) is always with you. You will have times to "mourn" or "grieve," but never let *"a spirit of grief"* attach itself to you. He carried our "griefs and sorrow"(Isaiah 53:4) so you won't have to. ♡♥♡

3-10

Beatitude #3

MATTHEW 5:5 NKJV *"Blessed are the meek, for they shall inherit the earth."*

Meek does not mean weak!! Meekness means teachable. We will always have new things to learn, so stay teachable! If we do, we will inherit – which is to be prosperous -- and "earth" means land. Did you ever see this one??? The Lord has blessings and prosperity for you as you stay teachable in His ways, you have an inheritance. ♡♥♡

3-11

Beatitude #4

MATTHEW 5:6 NKJV *"Blessed are those who hunger and thirst for righteousness, for they shall be filled."*

Stay hungry my friend – yes, for His Word, hunger and thirst for His Righteousness. By taking in the Word, your spiritual appetite grows. (Continued on the next page)

(Continued from previous page)
Physically and spiritually, you start with milk and progress in nourishment to sustain your maturing growth. Be a spiritual 'glutton' – every time, He promises that He will fill you up!! ♡♥♡

3-12
Beatitude #5

MATTHEW 5:7 NKJV *"Blessed are the merciful, for they shall obtain mercy."*
'Mercy' is grace in action. Jesus showed us mercy when we certainly did not deserve it. The principle of sowing and reaping is the example – you get what you sow. Sow some mercy today! You may need to reap it tomorrow. ♡♥♡

3-13
Beatitude #6

MATTHEW 5:8 NKJV *"Blessed are the pure in heart, for they shall see God."*
See the progression of these beatitudes? See the maturity that is progressive as we walk with Him? You *have* to walk in forgiveness to achieve the level of being "pure in heart." This maturing step brings you to a place you can "see God," or spiritually "perceive" God's plan for you. Your spiritual eyes enable you to understand what He is leading you into. ♡♥♡

3-14
Beatitude #7

MATTHEW 5:9 NKJV *"Blessed are the peacemakers, for they shall be called sons of God."*
God's peace sets us apart from other "religions." When you are full of God's love, you will walk in peace and bring His peace into any situation. "Sons of God" – you are God's "love child" and that is an endearing label. As you act like God acts, you earn the reputation of being part of His family. ♡♥♡

3-15
Beatitude #8

MATTHEW 5:10 NKJV *"Blessed are you who are persecuted for righteousness' sake, for theirs is the kingdom of heaven."*
Spiritual maturity enables you to rejoice even in tough times. "For righteousness' sake" are three important words – you are not blessed (happy, jubilant) just for any reason – but when you are put down by upholding His righteous standard a blessing follows. Choosing to do the "right thing" is always the best choice! ♡♥♡

3-16
*We will begin focusing on Jesus' last days before the crucifixion and the resurrection. These two events are cornerstones of Christianity.

LUKE 22:43 NKJV *"Then the angel appeared to Him from heaven, strengthening Him."*
Jesus was praying in the garden only a few hours before he was arrested. This should be a pattern we follow – to pray about every situation. Prayer will release angels to make things happen and answer our prayers. As you pray, you will be strengthened spiritually as well as physically. ♡♥♡

3-17
JOHN 18:6 NKJV *"Now when He said to them, "I am He," they drew back and fell to the ground."*
A large crowd including Judas, a detachment of troops, and officers from the chief priests and Pharisees (verse 3) came to the garden to arrest Jesus. When Jesus admitted He was Jesus of Nazareth, the power of His words caused the crowd to fall down to the ground! You would think that would be enough to let them know Jesus WAS who He said He was. Hate drives people to ignore the truth and pursue evil. Your words are containers of power. Your words literally frame your world. Use them wisely. ♡♥♡

3-18

JOHN 18:10 NLT *"Then Simon Peter drew a sword and slashed off the right ear of Malchus, the high priest's slave."*
I don't believe Peter was aiming for the ear – he was aiming for his head! The disciples feared for their lives and Peter was trying to defend Jesus. (Like Jesus needed defending!) But what were twelve men against such a huge armed crowd? Peter acted before thinking; can you relate??? ♡♥♡

3-19

LUKE 22:51 NLT *"But Jesus said, "No more of this." And He touched the man's ear and healed him."*
The beauty of this event (see yesterday's verse) was that Jesus reached down, picked up the ear, reattached it and healed it. Again, in their hate against Jesus, they ignored this miracle and pursued their agenda of hate. Love responded. ♡♥♡

3-20

MATTHEW 26:53 NLT *"Don't you realize that I could ask My Father for thousands (12 legions) of angels to protect us and He would send them instantly?"*
Jesus had already prayed in the garden and totally surrendered to His Father's will. HE knew the angelic hosts of heaven were at His disposal, but He chose to fulfill every detail of God's Redemption Plan for us. I am so grateful for His unselfishness. ♡♥♡

3-21

MATTHEW 26:56 NLT *"But this is all happening to fulfill the words of the prophets as recorded in the Scriptures." At that point, all the disciples deserted Him and fled."*
Thousands of years of prophecies were being fulfilled…think about how God is so organized and precise! With all the mentoring Jesus invested in his disciples, they ALL left Him when He needed them the most. That was pain upon pain, but Jesus endured it for us. ♡♥♡

3-22

MATTHEW 26:67 NLT *"Then they began to spit in Jesus' face and beat Him with their fists. And some slapped Him."*
Jesus is standing before the high priest Caiaphas with scribes and elders eager to find a way to kill Him because of jealousy and hate. Jesus hadn't been sentenced yet, but the crowd physically started abusing Him - illegally. Love bore it for us, so we can have His example to know the end result will be worth any shame. ♡♥♡

3-23

LUKE 22:64 NLT *"They blindfolded Him and said, "Prophesy to us! Who hit you that time?"*
The Roman military had a reputation of their cruelty to humanity. I personally can't fathom being cruel to a human (I can't watch any kind of movie or documentary about this subject). Stop a minute and just envision this scene, the mockery, the brutality, and Jesus silently taking it all…for you and me. Love endures. ♡♥♡

3-24

MATTHEW 27:2 NLT *"Then they bound Him, led Him away, and took Him to Pilate, the Roman governor."*
The politics of these two leaders went back and forth. Neither Herod nor Pilate wanted the responsibility of sentencing Jesus to death. This ordeal was going on all through the night – Jesus was taken into custody after 6:00 p.m. and escorted back and forth for twelve - fourteen hours. Sleep deprived, beaten, mocked, tortured; Jesus took it all, without saying a word. What love!!!! ♡♥♡

3-25

MATTHEW 27:11C, 12B, 14A NLT *"…Jesus replied, "You have said it." "…Jesus remained silent." "But Jesus made no response…."*
According to the Roman law, Jesus was given three opportunities to defend Himself. Each time, He remained silent. He had already prayed in the garden and He was obedient to God's plan. May the Lord give us ears to hear what God's plan is for our lives, a heart to understand and the willingness to follow it. ♡♥♡

3-26

LUKE 23:8 NLT *"Herod was delighted at the opportunity to see Jesus, because He had heard about Him and had been hoping for a long time to see Him perform a miracle."*
Political diplomats had heard of Jesus. His reputation preceded Him. Does your reputation precede you? Your prayers you pray for others open doors for the miraculous to work in your life. They will know us by our 'fruit.' Be 'fruitful' my friend! ♡♥♡

3-27

LUKE 23:15 NLT *"…(Pilate said) Nothing this man has done calls for the death penalty."*
Pilate saw through the sham of the religious leaders who were trying to get rid of Jesus. Pilate made sure the crowd knew he didn't see any reason for the death penalty, but he was too wimpy to stand up against them. Don't ever allow peer pressure to force you to do the "wrong thing." It takes true 'guts' to stand up for what is right. ♡♥♡

3-28

MATTHEW 27:26 NLT *"So Pilate released Barabbas to them. He ordered Jesus flogged with a lead-tipped whip, then turned Him over to the Roman soldiers to be crucified."*
What a travesty of justice. A convicted murderer set free and a totally innocent man tortured and murdered. But Jesus did all for us to fulfill the prophecies. Stripes were placed on His back for the healing of our bodies and minds. His death paid for all our sins – He was our blood sacrifice. Oh what a Savior!!!! ♡♥♡

3-29

MATTHEW 27:29 NLT *"They wove thorn branches into a crown and put it on His head…."*
Thorn bushes in Israel produce 2 inch thorns. When they shoved this "crown" on Jesus' head to mock Him –"the chastisement of our peace was upon Him" (Isaiah 53:5). He took all mental illnesses, headaches, etc. on Himself – for us. He gave us a sound mind!
(Continued on the next page)

28

(Continued from previous page)
We are not weak-minded or emotional wrecks. Jesus took all mental problems as well in this Redemption Plan. Take and receive everything Jesus paid the price for you to enjoy and fulfill your life. ♡♥♡

3-30

MATTHEW 27:33 NLT *"And they went out to a place called Golgotha (which means "Place of the Skull").*
In photographs of Golgotha, the rock formations resemble a human skull. It was not just a coincidence that was where He was crucified. Nothing in Jesus' crucifixion process was by "chance." Every detail fulfilled the Law and prophecies given thousands of years before this event. Nothing in your life is insignificant either. You are very special to God. Know that the Lord has every detail of your life planned out and great things are yours to enjoy! ♡♥♡

3-31

MATTHEW 27:35 NLT *"After they had nailed Him to the cross, the soldiers gambled for his clothes by throwing dice."*
The act of gambling for Jesus' robe fulfilled the prophecy in Psalm 22:18. Some people categorize Jesus as poor and weak. Only a very strong man could have endured the beatings, flogging, and crucifixion torture. The soldiers gambled for His robe because it was a very costly garment. This act of gambling at the foot of His cross was so irreverent and a mockery – a good argument point to resist gambling on any level today. ♡♥♡

APRIL

4-1

PHILIPPIANS 2:8 NLT *"He humbled Himself in obedience to God and died a criminal's death on the cross."*
The humility and meekness Jesus showed throughout His earthly life was a compelling example for us to follow. Things don't always go as we plan, tough times come, but as we are faithful to trust God throughout life, HE will guide us and provide everything we need. Even if you get wrongly accused, your Father God will be your defense. ♡♥♡

4-2

I PETER 1:18, 19 NLT *"Christ suffered for our sins once for all time. He never sinned, but He died for sinners to bring you safely home to God. He suffered physical death, but He was raised to life in the Spirit."*
Peter knew first-hand how Jesus completely fulfilled every part of the Jewish law and sacrifice for sins. In this scripture, Peter stated it so plainly. Jesus was sinless but carried all our sin to give us our "pathway" HOME to God the Father. ♡♥♡

4-3

JOHN 19:30 NLT *"...He said, 'It is finished!' Then He bowed His head and released His spirit."* (Also Matthew 27:50)
I love this verse. When Jesus said, "It is finished," the sacrifice for our sins was literally complete. Jesus fulfilled every jot and tittle of The Law – so we would never have to. HE made it so simple – Believe on Him and you will have eternal life! He knew the exact time, and Jesus gave His life – the soldiers did not take His life – He freely and willingly released His spirit to our Father God. ♡♥♡

4-4

MATTHEW 27:51 NLT *"At that moment the curtain in the sanctuary of the temple was torn in two, from top to bottom...."*
This scripture is so very important to know how Jesus' blood bought back humanity from Adam's fall. Now we can come personally before God – no more need for a mediator (priest) to go into His presence for us - but we can come boldly into His presence. The curtain was torn from Top to Bottom – indicating God did it (the curtain was known to be about 4 inches thick). Humans could not have done that! God desires to talk to you personally. Spend time daily with Him!! ♡♥♡

4-5

JOHN 19:41, 42 NLT *"The place of crucifixion was near a garden, where there was a new tomb never used before...they laid Jesus there."*
When Jesus' life was completed, His body was buried in a new tomb nearby. This burial site was new – and I like to say it remained unused, since Jesus' spirit went to hell for us and completely conquered the devil for 3 days and 3 nights as prophesied (Matthew 12:40). I know we have been taught and our calendar says Jesus was crucified Friday and raised on Sunday – but you can't scripturally get three days and three nights in that time frame. I'll stick with The Word and not the 'traditions' or calendar.... ♡♥♡

4-6

MATTHEW 28:2 NLT *"Suddenly there was a great earthquake! For an angel of the Lord came down from heaven, rolled aside the stone, and sat on it."*
When Jesus died on the cross, an earthquake occurred (Matthew 27:51). Here, when the angel came and rolled away the huge stone at the opening of His tomb, there was another earthquake. The glory of God is powerful and earth shaking! ♡♥♡

4-7

MARK 16:2-4 NLT *"Very early on Sunday morning (first day of the week) just at sunrise, they went to the tomb.... But as they arrived, they looked up and saw that stone...had already been rolled aside."*
The three women came early to the tomb and were even discussing how they would get into the tomb. They were going to prepare His body since the Sabbath was over. Little did they know an angel came ahead of them and the tomb was EMPTY! Because He lives...we live!!!! ♡♥♡

4-8

LUKE 24:6, 7 NLT *"He isn't here! He is risen from the dead! Remember what He told you back in Galilee saying, 'The Son of Man must be delivered into the hands of sinful men, and be crucified, and the third day rise again'."*
Two angels reminded the women what Jesus had told them about what His mission was. The fulfillment of His Word became reality. There is no way, other than God, that Old and New Testament prophecies about Jesus could "just happen". Jesus is alive!!! He is risen!! He is living proof God's Word is truth!! ♡♥♡

4-9

MATTHEW 28:18-20 NLT *"Teach these new disciples to obey all the commandments I have given you. And be sure of this; I Am with you always, even to the end of the age."*
Jesus remained on earth 40 days after His resurrection. He revealed Himself to many. Jesus' final instruction to His followers was to obey His WORD. Personally reading and studying His Word should be an ongoing, daily activity and to share His Word with others. There is always more to learn and experience in and through His Word. Jesus' closing remarks were of comfort and encouragement – He will ALWAYS be with us – you are NEVER alone!!! You are well-loved!! ♡♥♡

4-10

LUKE 24:51 NLT *"While He was blessing them He was taken up to heaven."*

Jesus' mode-of-operation is to bless. The last thing He did on this earth was to bless the people. As He was releasing blessings, He departed and went back to His Father in heaven. Don't ever get the idea God and Jesus are just out to harm or hurt you in any way. Everything Jesus did on the earth was to do good; He was moved by compassion, He healed, and provided for His followers. He is still doing that today. Seek Jesus as your source. God NEVER fails us! ♡♥♡

4-11

EPHESIANS 2:14 NLT *"For Christ Himself has brought peace to us. He united Jews and Gentiles into one people when, in his own body on the cross, He broke down the wall of hostility that separated us."*

Paul refers to the Holy of Holies curtain being eradicated by God (see 4-4). Our Heavenly Father desires all mankind be united by Jesus. Jealousy, anger, prejudice, bitterness, etc., divide – God's heart is for all to walk in peace and love for each other. We can walk out all Jesus paid for us by showing His love toward others. ♡♥♡

4-12

HEBREWS 19:20 NLT *"Now may the God of peace – who brought up from the dead our Lord Jesus, the great Shepherd of the sheep, and ratified an eternal covenant with His blood...."*

I am emphasizing this thought – Jesus purchased the eternal covenant for us to walk in peace and love toward others. I believe in the days we live, the love of God toward others will win souls for the Kingdom!!! Walk in love today! ♡♥♡

4-13

PSALM 78:4 NKJV *"...telling to the generation to come the praises of the Lord...."*

It is so very important that we pass along to the next generation our heritage in the Lord. (Continued on the next page)

(Continued from previous page)
It's not enough to just teach them, but to live the example before them, so they can see how the things of God are the real deal. ♡♥♡

4-14

JOHN 20:29 NKJV *"...Blessed are those who have not seen and yet have believed."*
Jesus was talking to Thomas in a conversation after His resurrection. We are the generation who believe by faith that Jesus truly is the Son of God. We believe by faith since we haven't seen Jesus in the flesh, but we believe His Word and His promises. We are blessed as we believe. ♡♥♡

4-15

PROVERBS 12:15 NLT *"Worry weighs a person down; an encouraging word cheers a person up."*
Today, even if you are weighed down by worries and troubles, reach out and share an encouraging compliment to someone else and see how refreshed you feel. As you give, encouragement will come back to you. Sowing and reaping works! ♡♥♡

4-16

DEUTERONOMY 32:4 NKJV *"HE is the Rock, His work is perfect; for all His ways are justice, a God of truth and without injustice; Righteous and upright is HE."*
We have to believe right to live right. As the scripture says, our God is the firm Rock you can always go to and find help. God IS right, His ways are right, His truth (Word) is right. As you seek Him, He will keep you safe, protected, etc. ♡♥♡

4-17

PSALM 4:8 MSG. *"At day's end I'm ready for sound sleep, for You, God, have put my life back together."*
As Christians, we are not immune from trouble times and situations. At times, we do get hurt, disappointed and discouraged. I find strength in this version. (Continued on the next page)

(Continued from previous page)
Only God can put us back together again. Regardless of how hard your situation may be - God can put your life back together!!!! Be encouraged today! ♡♥♡

4-18

SONG OF SOLOMON 4:7 MSG. *"You're beautiful from head to toe, my dear love, beautiful beyond compare, absolutely flawless."*
Do you see yourself the way God sees you? This verse expresses how HE sees you. God loves you so much – HE sees you "in Christ" and we need to see ourselves "in Him" – beautiful and flawless! No we are not perfect – but we are forgiven! ♡♥♡

4-19

JOB 34:10 MSG. *"It is impossible for God to do anything evil; no way can the Mighty One do wrong."*
There is never a reason to blame God for evil. We need to pay attention to this scripture because God is always for us and He desires the best for us. Always run to God when things get tough – He can change your situation and bring you out stronger than ever. Don't run from God – run to Him! ♡♥♡

4-20

JOB 42:5, 6 MSG. *"I admit I once lived by rumors of You, now I have it all firsthand – from my own eyes and ears! I'm sorry - forgive me. I'll never do that again, I promise! I'll never again live on crusts of hearsay, crumbs of rumor."*
By the end of the book of Job, he comes to the Truth. Job searched for God and the truth through friends, but we can know God personally through His Word and in prayer. We can know God firsthand, personally, intimately!!! Spend time with Him today. HE loves you so very much! ♡♥♡

4-21

PROVERBS 15:4 MSG. *"Kind words heal and help; cutting words wound and maim."*
We know how to frame our world by speaking God's Word over our lives, but have you thought about how you can encourage others by the words you speak to them? You never know what other people are going through, but just a kind word can change their day. Choose your words carefully and be an encouragement to others today. It doesn't cost you anything monetarily, but you can lift others up which is priceless!!!! ♡♥♡

4-22

EPHESIANS 4:1 MSG. *"In light of all this, here's what I want you to do. While I'm locked up here, a prisoner for the Master, I want you to get out there and walk – better yet, run! – on the road God called you to travel. I don't want any of you sitting around on your hands...."*
Paul is really encouraging us to find out what God has called us to do and get after it. You have Divine giftings and God needs you to fulfill your destiny. It's exciting times, so don't pull back, but press in and be "all in" for Him. ♡♥♡

4-23

HEBREWS 10:35-39 MSG. *"...But you need to stick it out, staying with God's plan so you'll be there for the promised completion.... But we're not quitters who lose out. Oh, no! We'll stay with it and survive, trusting all the way."*
The writer of Hebrews is God's cheerleader encouraging us on to stay with God's plan for our lives. Jesus is certainly coming soon, so don't quit now – you are a vital part of the end time harvest!! ♡♥♡

4-24

JAMES 2:1 MSG. *"My dear friends, don't let public opinion influence how you live out our glorious, Christ-originated faith."*
In these days, political correctness often dilutes issues. It seems like everything is a grey area, no real right or wrong. James is saying for us to stick with God's Word. This is a sure thing! People's opinions are not the issue - staying with The Word is the issue. Live to please God, do not live to please people! ♡♥♡

4-25

I THESSALONIANS 5:23, 24 MSG. *"May God Himself, the God who makes everything holy and whole, make you holy and whole, put you together—spirit, soul, and body—and keep you fit for the coming of our Master, Jesus Christ. The One who called you is completely dependable. If He said it, He'll do it!"*
WOW what a word from God! He can put you back together from a broken heart, physical loss, addictions, etc. Only God can do that. HE desires to make us complete in Him – spiritually, physically and mentally. Spend time with Him, so He can put your pieces back together again and make you whole. ♡♥♡

4-26

I TIMOTHY 2:1 MSG. *"The first thing I want you to do is pray. Pray every way you know how, for everyone you know. Pray especially for rulers and their governments to rule well so we can be quietly about our business of living simply in humble contemplation."*
It doesn't cost any money to pray – only time. This is something everyone can and should be doing. We can pray and we can vote and believe God to move and guide our leaders to lead righteously. Pray for their salvation and wisdom. Take a little time every day to pray over your family, co-workers, government, elected and appointed leaders. ♡♥♡

4-27

HEBREWS 1:1 MSG. *"The fundamental fact of existence is that this trust in God, this faith, is the firm foundation under everything that makes life worth living. It's our handle on what we can't see."*
Faith is the bedrock of our belief in the True God. As we believe in Jesus and all HE did for us, it's all by faith—faith in The Word. Your faith is exercised and increases as you hear, study, meditate on The Word. Faith is not automatic! YOU have a part to play. Be diligent and exercise your faith daily, your faith will grow, act on your faith and see God working through you and prayers answered. ♡♥♡

4-28

I CORINTHIANS 12:26 MSG. *"You are Christ's body—that's who you are! You must never forget this. Only as you accept your part of that body does your "part" mean anything."*
The family of God is called "the body of Christ." We are "in Him," finding our place and doing what He calls us to. As Paul says – never forget this. You are not a "Lone Ranger" in the family of God – you have a vast network of brothers and sisters joining with you. Greater than that – God's life gives us strength, peace, safety – there is nothing you lack when you abide "in Him", in His body. ♡♥♡

4-29

PHILIPPIANS 4:13 MSG. *"Whatever I have, wherever I am, I can make it through anything in the One who makes me who I am."*
"Contentment" is a wonderful place to be. It is miserable to be in a state of always wanting more and not reaching it. Our success or contentment is not in "things", it is "in Him". HE truly is our everything. We are complete "in Him". I believe a key to contentment is to be at rest in Him, knowing He freely gives us everything we need. We are His "love children". You are well-loved by God! ♡♥♡

4-30

PHILIPPIANS 4:6,7 MSG. *"Don't fret or worry. Instead of worrying, pray. Let petitions and praises <u>shape your worries into prayers</u>, letting God know your concerns. Before you know it, a sense of God's wholeness, everything coming together for good, will come and settle you down. It's wonderful what happens when Christ displaces worry at the center of your life."*

There's not much to expound on this verse - it says it all. Worry is such a waste of time about things that are in the future that haven't happened yet. Be worry-free because "God's got this". Trust Him by shaping/exchanging those worries to prayer and praise today. ♡♥♡

MAY

5-1

PSALM 94:14, 15 MSG. *"God will never walk away from His people, never desert His precious people. Rest assured that justice is on its way and every good heart put right."*
Don't ever listen to the devil's lie that God doesn't care about you. Your Heavenly Father loves everything about you! You are precious! Only HE can make wrongs right. God is for you, not against you. Trust Him! ♡♥♡

5-2

HEBREWS 2:9 MSG. *"In that death, by God's grace, he fully experienced death in every person's place."*
We should see our sins nailed to the cross with Jesus paying the price just like we know that in baptism we were buried with Him AND raised with Him. Jesus truly experienced it all for us. HE died in our place, so we can LIVE in Him. ♡♥♡

5-3

MATTHEW 5:22 MSG. *"The simple moral fact is that words kill."*
Our words build the frame for our lives. Watch over what comes out of your mouth because words are powerful! Have encouraging words for yourself, your co-workers, family members, etc. Words produce life or death. As you sow, you will reap. ♡♥♡

5-4

JAMES 4:7B KJV *"...Resist the devil and he will flee from you."*
We know the devil is already defeated, so why give him any attention? The BEST way to resist the devil is to ignore him, or better yet – laugh at him. Any thought that comes to us that contradicts the Truth (The Word), simply ignore it; don't give it any entrance. The devil will pass on to someone else who will listen to his lies. Resist/ignore the devil and he will move on! ♡♥♡

5-5

EPHESIANS 1:6B KJV *"...He has made us accepted in the Beloved."*
The word "accepted" in the Greek is *"charitoo"* which means highly favored. This word is used only one other time - when the angel appeared to Mary that she would bear God's Son. God loves you because you are His love child...not for anything you have done, but whose you are! Today lift up your head, believe and know you are highly favored of your Father God. He desires to bless and promote you today. ♡♥♡

5-6

ROMANS 8:32 NLT *"Since HE (God) did not spare even His own Son but gave Him (Jesus) up for us all, won't He also give us everything else?"*
God's love for us is totally true. Jesus' obedience to The Father brought us into a position 'in Him.' As we see ourselves "in Him", we have ALL THINGS we need and in abundance. Our success is a direct result of being objects of HIS love. HE freely gives it to us, we don't have to beg and plead for it, HE is freely giving out His blessing! God is so in love with you...receive it and enjoy! ♡♥♡

5-7

EXODUS 14:13 NKJV *"...Do not be afraid. Stand still, and see the salvation of the Lord...."*
The Hebrew word for 'salvation' is *"yeshua"* which means salvation is the person of Jesus! Sometimes our situations are so big, we can't see how they can be fixed. But as you see Jesus as your 'salvation,' your answer, your deliverer, your supplier to fix your situation, you can stand still and watch Him work it out on your behalf. ♡♥♡

5-8

PSALM 90:14 NKJV *"Oh, satisfy us early with Your mercy, that we may rejoice and be glad all our days!"*
Mercy means God's grace.   (Continued on the next page)

(Continued from previous page)

The Hebrew word *"hesed"* here means God's grace, love, tender mercies and lovingkindness. Be satisfied with God's mercy today. You have everything you need in His mercy.

It's not something you have to earn, it is in fully supplied your relationship with Him. Draw close to Him early and let Him bless you today. ♡♥♡

5-9

II CHRONICLES 20:20C NKJV *"...Believe in the Lord your God, and you shall be established; believe His prophets, and you shall prosper."*
I'm going to take a few days to break this verse down because it is so important.

"Believe in the Lord your God." What you believe is so very important. What you believe will shape your life. Think about what you believe, is it because someone you love believes it, or do you believe it because God's Word says it? As Joseph Prince says, "If you believe right, you will live right." The Word should be the basis of our beliefs. ♡♥♡

5-10

II CHRONICLES 20:20C NKJV *"...Believe in the Lord your God...."*
Yesterday, we explored your believing. Today let's look at the God you should believe in. You are to *'believe in the Lord YOUR God'*. You cannot live on your parent's, or grandparent's, etc., God - but you have the responsibility to have your personal relationship with your Lord. Is HE your God? Do you know Him? Do you talk with Him? How close is your relationship with your God? He desires to be very personal and very close to you. ♡♥♡

5-11

II CHRONICLES 20:20C NKJV *"...Believe in the Lord your God, **and you shall be established**; believe His prophets, and you shall prosper"*.
The Lord will establish you. (Continued on the next page)

(Continued from previous page)

"Establish" is *amam* in Hebrew - to build up or support; to foster as a parent or nurse; to render firm or faithful. The Lord will cause you to have a firm foundation to build your life on. HE is your faithful Father God and you are His love child. Re-read how the Lord "establishes" you. You are in GOOD hands for sure! ♡♥♡

5-12

II CHRONICLES 20:20C NKJV *"...Believe in the Lord your God, and you shall be established; believe His prophets, and you shall prosper."* Prophets – *nabiy* are "inspired ones". In today's society, there are many television programs that will certainly inspire you with The Word. However, nothing takes the place of finding your place in a local church. Being "planted" in a church gives you a spiritual covering. Everyone needs to find a Godly pastor who preaches/teaches the Word. The Word of God is information, inspiration and revelation. I thank God for the many people I credit for inspiring me in my walk. ♡♥♡

5-13

II CHRONICLES 20:20C NKJV *"...Believe in the Lord your God, and you shall be established; believe His prophets, and so shall you prosper."*
God is a good God. *'..and so shall you prosper'* - He always wants to "prosper" us; *tsalach* – to push forward, break out, come mightily, go over, be good, be meek, be profitable. Only as His prophets teach His Word and we obey the Word will we truly prosper. The Word has a "Blessing" attached to IT as we hear and obey IT. ♡♥♡

5-14

MARK 11:25, 26 GNB *"And when you stand and pray, forgive anything you have against anyone, so that your Father in Heaven will forgive the wrongs you have done."*

(Continued on the next page)

(Continued from previous page)

So if we don't forgive, our prayers will not be answered - a very dangerous place to be. It is only when we forgive and "let it go" are we truly free. Don't let unforgiveness keep you from getting answers to prayer. ♡♥♡

5-15

MATTHEW 6:12 KJV *"...Forgive us our debts, as we forgive our debtors."*

This verse is not just talking about money. When someone has hurt you, not always physically or financially, but emotionally, we might feel that person owes us something. Unforgiveness does not affect the other person, it affects you! Being mad at a person only affects you! Jesus told us to forgive them and let it go!! As you forgive, you will see that opens an avenue for God to heal and bless you like no one else can. ♡♥♡

5-16

HEBREWS 10:23 NLT *"Let us come into agreement with God and begin to speak what He says, tightly wrapping our arms around the promise we are confessing - embracing it with all our might, holding tightly to it, rejecting all attempts of anyone who tries to steal it from us, not allowing ourselves to be fickle in our commitment, but determined in what we believe and confess in faith... All things are possible to them that believe."*

We are familiar with the last sentence, but there are some prerequisites to fulfill before we acquire those results. It's not enough just to know the Word, we must confess the Word as well. Your words are powerful. God's Word is the ultimate power. As you confess His Word, God will back His Word. ♡♥♡

5-17

PSALM 138:2B KJV *"...for thou hast magnified thy word above all thy name."*

(Continued on the next page)

(Continued from previous page)

Circumstances can never change the promises of God - but the promises of God can change circumstances. Heaven and earth will pass away, but God's Word will never change. Make the Word of God the foundation of your life.♡♥♡

5-18

EPHESIANS 3:16-17 KJV *"That He would grant you, according to the riches of His glory, to be strengthened with might by His Spirit in the inner man. That Christ may dwell in your hearts by faith; that you, being rooted and grounded in love...."*
You should pray this prayer in Ephesians every day. Just pray The Word. God's Word has power and as we speak it over ourselves, His power is infused in us. ♡♥♡

5-19

Prayer for wisdom **Ephesians 1:15-23** (use whatever version you like).
EPHESIANS 1:17 KJV *"That the God of our Lord Jesus Christ, the Father of glory, may give you the <u>spirit of wisdom</u>...."*
We need God's wisdom every day for every situation. Through Jesus, we have the wisdom of God at our disposal; all we have to do is ask for it! We can have "inside information" if we just ask and listen. Look at this entire chapter. Better yet, pray this chapter daily and see God's wisdom increase in your life. ♡♥♡

5-20

MATTHEW 6:31 KJV *"Therefore <u>take no thought</u>, <u>saying</u>...."*
We have to take control of our thoughts as well as our mouths. People don't know what you are thinking about UNTIL you open your mouth. Many thoughts come through our brains throughout the day. We have control whether we just let them go on through and out, or actually take possession of the thought by SAYING or speaking it. Our words are a creative force, so choose your words wisely my friend. ♡♥♡

5-21

GALATIANS 5:6 NKJV *"...but faith working through love"*.
Faith grows in the atmosphere of love. God literally IS Love. Faith becomes a dominating and creative force when Love really rules. No love – no faith. Faith won't work without love. To walk in love is actually to live in the faith of God. ♡♥♡

5-22

JOHN 15:7 MSG. *"But if you make yourselves at home with Me and My Words are at home with you, you can be sure that whatever you ask will be listened to and acted upon."*
What an encouraging scripture and instruction for us. Prayer is simply talking to God. We don't have to use King James English to talk to God. Prayer can even be reminding God of His Word and let Him know you believe Him. It is vital as you know Him, you "make yourself at home" with Him. Reread this scripture again. ♡♥♡

5-23

LAMENTATIONS 3:25 NKJV *"The Lord is good to those who wait for Him, to the soul who seeks Him."*
There aren't very many "uplifting verses" in this book of the Bible. If you look at a situation, person, etc., long enough, you can find something good. This verse lets us know as you wait - minister to the Lord (waiting is not just doing nothing, it is ministering, praising and worshipping God), HE will cause good plans, situations, blessings to come your way. Those that look to Him, seek out His ways will be well taken care of. He is such a good Heavenly Father and He is really interested in the details of your life as well. ♡♥♡

5-24

JUDE 21 KJV *"...keep yourselves in the love of God...."*
I can't improve on this statement from a great man of God, E.W. Kenyon -"If we live in God's love, we begin to bear fruits of love. The fruit of LOVE will be in actions and the conduct and the words that are born of love." Your life IS a witness! No words necessary.... ♡♥♡

5-25

PROVERBS 25:15 AMP *"By long forbearance and calmness of spirit a judge or ruler is persuaded, and soft speech breaks down the most bonelike resistance."*
You may be in a hard situation right now, but things WILL change. Keep your spirit calm and trust God. Choose your words and actions wisely and watch God put things together as only HE can. ♡♥♡

5-26

I CORINTHIANS 13:8A KJV *"Love NEVER fails...."*
You can get more accomplished in an atmosphere of LOVE. So today, let God's love rule you in every area of your thinking and life. All we think and do and say born of LOVE is pleasant, peaceful and positive. "Never" is a very strong word, but when God says His "agape" love will never fail, it will <u>never</u> <u>fail</u>.♡♥♡

5-27

LUKE 11:9B KJV *"...SEEK and you will find...."*
If you seek the help of the Lord, He will show you what to do in every situation. So ask the Holy Spirit today to give you the mind of Christ for every situation that is presented to you. Seek Him because He desires to help you. ♡♥♡

5-28

PSALM 92:10B NKJV *"...I have been anointed with fresh oil."*
David knew he needed a fresh, <u>now</u>, daily blessing from the Lord. Just like David, we are to desire the hand of the Lord on our life daily with a freshness that will empower us and make us a blessing to the people we are around. ♡♥♡

5-29

NAHUM 1:7 NLT *"The Lord is good, a strong refuge when trouble comes, He is close to those who trust in Him."*
What a promise for today! God IS good; HE is our strength for today. Run to Him today. Don't run from Him. HE is your help. He is the way of escape! ♡♥♡

5-30

MICAH 7:8 KJV *"Rejoice not against me, O mine enemy (the devil); when I fall, I shall arise; when I sit in darkness, the Lord shall be a light unto me."*
Whatever trial you go through - the Lord is WITH you and will bring you out victorious!! Keep a thankful heart and keep your JOY level up by going and spending time with Jesus – in His Presence, there is fullness of joy! He is your light in the dark place you may be in, but you're coming out victorious!!!! ♡♥♡

5-31

GENESIS 17:2 NKJV *"And I will make My covenant between Me and you, and will multiply you exceedingly."*
I want to tell you something and don't ever forget it: when you are born again, you're a covenant Child of God! You have rights, and privileges. What affects you affects God. HE will always defend and protect you! ♡♥♡

JUNE

6-1

ROMANS 12:21AMP *"Do not let yourself be overcome by evil, but overcome (master) evil with GOOD. Just because some people don't walk in love and are angry, be the bigger person - act and react in love. LOVE NEVER FAILS."*

You don't have to look too hard to see how anger and hate dominate this world. As Believers, we operate on a higher level. Let His Love dominate you and you will be an Overcomer in every situation. You are overcoming in life's situations by walking in love. ♡♥♡

6-2

I PETER 1:8 AMP *"Without having seen Him, you love Him; …you believe in Him and exult and thrill with inexpressible and glorious (triumphant, heavenly) joy."*

If you lose your joy, the devil gets a stronghold in your life. When Jesus is your focus, as you go daily into His Presence – there is fullness of joy to keep your "joy tank" full. When you get to feeling "down" go into His presence for a "fill up"! ♡♥♡

6-3

PSALM 33:1 AMP *"Rejoice in the Lord, O you [uncompromisingly] righteous [you upright, in right standing with God]; for praise is becoming and appropriate for those who are upright [in heart]."*

PRAISE is a powerful and effective weapon to defeat the devil. Use it daily! Praise will lift your emotions and bring you into victory. ♡♥♡

6-4

I THESSALONIANS 1:3 KJV *"Remembering without ceasing your work of **faith**, and labour of love, and **patience** of hope in our Lord Jesus Christ...."*
Paul's letter to the church in Thessalonica was encouraging in the fact Paul was thinking of how faithful they had been.
Kenneth Copeland says, "<u>Faith</u> opens the door to God's promise for you; and <u>patience</u> keeps it open until that promise is fulfilled."
<u>Faith</u> and <u>patience</u> are two powerful forces that will keep you balanced. When you pray, you believe you receive your answer then, patience will keep you in a position to receive the answer until it comes. Use these two powerful 'twins'. ♡♥♡

6-5

2 COR.12:9 NKJV *"And HE said unto me, "MY grace is sufficient for you, for MY strength is made perfect in weakness."*
When we get to the end of our abilities - God steps in and helps us get through anything we are facing. God's grace will keep you in a place to receive.♡♥♡

6-6

ISAIAH 40:31 AMP*"But those who wait for the Lord [who expect, look for, and hope in Him] shall change and renew their strength and power"* (the power to overcome adversity).
You are more than a conqueror in Jesus.
While you are waiting (actively trusting)...God is working!! ♡♥♡

Ella C. Brunt

6-7

ROMANS 12:21 AMP *"Do not let yourself be overcome by evil, but overcome (master) evil with good."*
When we have been wronged, it is so easy to try to get back at that person. We must stop and recognize who is behind the evil and know God will vindicate us if we act with good and defeat the evil. It takes more self-control to act and not <u>react</u>. ♡♥♡

6-8

I SAMUEL 2:1 NLT *"My heart rejoices in the Lord! The Lord has made me strong. Now I have an answer for my enemies; I rejoice because You rescued me."*
As YOU rejoice and give the Lord thanksgiving, HE will give you strength in your life. HE will also give you His wisdom and answers only HE can give you. And yes, HE will rescue us out of many traps the devil would love to use to distract and hurt us. All these benefits come by rejoicing and spending time with HIM. ♡♥♡

6-9

EPHESIANS 3:20 NKJV *"God is able to do exceedingly abundantly above all that we ask or think."*
I don't know about you, but I have a big imagination.... But God has a bigger one! HE is able and willing to give us ALL good things. You are a King's kid so get ready to receive His overflowing blessings today! ♡♥♡

6-10

DANIEL 11:32B KJV *"...but the people that do know their God shall be strong, and do exploits."*
The most important thing we can do is to draw close and continually strive to really KNOW GOD. HE has given us His Word to reveal Himself personally to us. Read the Word daily, pray and put Him first in everything you do. In doing, you will be equipped to do great exploits!!!!! How exciting!!! ♡♥♡

6-11

3 JOHN 2 KJV *"Beloved, I wish above all things that thou mayest prosper and be in health, even as thy soul (your mind, will and emotions) prospers."*
God wants us healthy, wealthy (we have more than what we need so we can give and bless others) and wise!!! Really, HE does!! HE wants us whole and functioning to our greatest potential. ♡♥♡

6-12

PSALM 34:8 KJV *"Oh taste and see that the Lord is good; blessed is the man that trusteth in Him."*
You'll never know just how good HE is until you get close. Put HIM first and top priority in everything. As you 'taste' and get close to Him, His GOODNESS will overwhelm you. ♡♥♡

6-13

PROVERBS 16:32 NKJV *"He who is slow to anger is better than the mighty, and he who rules his spirit than he who takes the city."*
Self-control is only possible when you stay full of the love of God by spending time with HIM. You are in charge of your emotions. You show strength when you can stop anger and not allow it to overtake you. You can do it! ♡♥♡

6-14

PSALM 16:1 NKJV *"Preserve me O God, for in You do I put my trust."*
Trust God when you don't know all the right answers to your questions and decisions. HE is working in you and preparing you for the answers and will reveal them when you are ready. Keep leaning on HIM - it pleases HIM. HE will keep you safe and protected. ♡♥♡

Ella C. Brunt

6-15

PSALM 34:15 NLT *"The eyes of the Lord watch over those who do right; His ears are open to their cries for help."*
Just think how much God loves you and desires to bless you and meet your EVERY need and desire!!! You are a child of the MOST HIGH GOD. God has eyes and ears that focus on you! He is listening for your call. Awesome, isn't He! ♡♥♡

6-16

JUDE 20 AMP *"But you, beloved, build up yourselves up [founded] on your most holy faith [make progress, rise like an edifice higher and higher], praying in the <u>Holy Spirit</u>."*
One way to grow and mature your spirit is to pray in tongues. God will impart to you wisdom, understanding, witty ideas, etc., that you need to get through situations you face. The Holy Spirit will pray the perfect will of God for your life every time. HE knows what you need and as you pray HE is enabled to bring it to you. Just like we work out physically to stay "fit" - we MUST pray in the Spirit every day to stay 'tuned in' and strong to live our lives to please God. ♡♥♡

6-17

PROVERBS 4:20A NKJV *"My son, give attention to My words...."*
*For the next several days we will look at three very important verses in Proverbs.
God is giving us instructions to pay attention to His Word. Don't be distracted by unimportant things in life. His Word *IS* <u>life</u> to you. Pay attention, give your attention to His Word. God will speak to you through the Bible. I've seen an acronym of the Bible as **B**-basic **I**-instructions **B**-before **L**-leaving **E**-earth! ♡♥♡

6-18

PROVERBS 4:20B NKJV *"...incline your ear to My sayings."*
Again, this is a commandment for us to obey, NOT a suggestion! We are to read and pay attention to His Word. We are to <u>listen</u> to <u>hear</u> His Word. LISTENING is an acquired skill.
(Continued on the next page)

(Continued from previous page)

You can hear with your physical ears, but HE wants us to be on the same wave length to actually <u>listen</u> to the message HE is speaking to us through His Word. Don't just read the words on the page, but let your heart/spirit <u>listen</u> what HE is saying to you. God wants a personal audience with you! ♡♥♡

6-19

PROVERBS 4:21A NKJV *"Do not let them depart from your eyes...."*
In this age of technology, there still is no stronger 'visual input' for us - than to actually READ His Word. The eye gate is one of several inputs for God to share His thoughts to get inside our minds/heart. Your phone has apps available, so wherever you and your phone are - you have access to read His Word/thoughts. Take time EVERYDAY to keep His Word before your eyes. There is no substitute for actually reading His Word! ♡♥♡

6-20

PROVERBS 4:21B NKJV *"Keep them (His Words) in the midst of your heart...."*
Again, God's Word should be highly treasured. HE puts so much importance to read and obey His Word because it <u>is</u> life and health to us. Whatever is dear and near to our hearts (the center of our lives), will chart our course in life. God desires that you value His Word. Put the Word in, so it can be our guide and the strength of our existence!! ♡♥♡

6-21

PROVERBS 4:22A NKJV *"For they are life to those who find them...."*
The Word of God IS life, so it gives life, strength, wisdom, peace, knowledge - whatever LIFE we need. His Word <u>is</u> <u>LIFE</u> to us. HE imparts HIS LIFE to us through HIS Word. And notice that it takes effort on our part. Treasure does not just sit out in the open! We have to put effort, time, and attention into His LIFE giving Word to uncover it. Seek and you will find! Dig in!!! ♡♥♡

56

6-22

PROVERBS 4:22B NKJV *"...and health to all your flesh."*

We have seen how there is no substitute for reading God's Word. We conclude this 3 verse study to see how the Word IS HEALTH to you. The Word accurately applied is RX or medicine to your body. Some Bibles have a reference by this verse to say 'medicine' for the word 'health'. You have to search it out, read, study, listen, and confess the Word and it has the power to change you and your situations. ♡♥♡

6-23

PSALM 28:7 NLT *"The Lord is my strength and shield (protection). I trust Him with all my heart. He helps me, and my heart is filled with joy, I burst out in songs of thanksgiving."*

Who do you trust? In life, we sometimes trust people and they disappoint us. When you give your heart to someone and they let you down, it leaves you emotionally hurt. The Lord will NEVER disappoint, fail, trick or deceive you. When you really KNOW Him, He becomes your "everything." Whatever you need - He is. You will lack nothing. David knew His God and sang this song because he knew the Lord on a very personal level. We can know Him on this level too. Spend time with Jesus; He wants you to REALLY know Him. ♡♥♡

6-24

MATTHEW 6:34 AMP *"So do not worry or be anxious about tomorrow, for tomorrow will have worries and anxieties of its own...."*

Just like you can't go through life looking in the rearview mirror about your past, you can't be worried about things that haven't happened yet either. Live for the NOW! We give our best for today and trust God for the rest. "Do not worry" is specific—don't do it! We are in great hands with Jesus! No worries then!!! ♡♥♡

6-25

PSALM 118:24 NKJV *"This is the day the Lord has made; We will rejoice and be glad in it."*
David certainly did not have a life without problems and challenges. This song reflects how attitudes determine your altitude and sets the stage for your day. Begin your day reflecting on God's goodness and choose to rejoice! We always have something we can praise God for. We live for TODAY because tomorrow is not promised. We make a choice to have a thankful heart. As you praise and rejoice in the Lord for His greatness, your attitude is lifted up.
In praise - we raise. Try it!!! ♡♥♡

6-26

ISAIAH 26:3 AMP *"You will guard me and keep me in perfect peace and constant peace as my mind (both its inclination and character) is stayed on YOU, because I commit myself to You, I lean on You, and confidently hope in You."*
The peace of God is not just a calm feeling. The Shalom peace is having your every need met, nothing missing and nothing lacking! Re-read this scripture and soak in how God watches over you. ♡♥♡

6-27

I TIMOTHY 6:17 NKJV *"…Who gives us richly all things to enjoy."*
Paul is writing to Timothy and says to trust in the living God. Our God is so loving and interested in us - HE wants us to enjoy life, not just barely get by and "exist." Today, realize God loves you soooo much and HE desires to bless you!!! I love you too! ♡♥♡

6-28

ROMANS 12:2 PHIL. *"Don't let the world around you squeeze you into its own mold but let God remold your minds from within…."*
When we are born again, our spirit changes from darkness to light. When Jesus becomes your Lord and Savior, your spirit is made alive to God. Up to that point and time, the world tries to label you, form you to "fit" in. God gives us His Word to 'mold' our thoughts and desires to please Him. ♡♥♡

6-29

I COR.13:7, 8 AMP *"Love bears up under anything and everything that comes, is ever ready to believe the best of every person, its hopes are fadeless under all circumstances, and it endures everything (without weakening). LOVE NEVER FAILS...."*

You can have all the faith in the world, but if LOVE isn't in the equation, it will not work. The world recognizes us as Christians by seeing and experiencing our love. Our human love is limited, but only the Love of God in us makes it possible. ♡♥♡

6-30

PSALM 139:14 NKJV *"I praise You, for I am fearfully and wonderfully made; marvelous are Your works...."*

You are not an "accident" or "insignificant." God has you here for a reason. You have a destiny to fulfill that no one else can do it. GOD is orchestrating and ordaining your life. Your mission in life is to stay pliable, teachable, and willing in God's hands – HE will orchestrate your life into things better than you could ever imagine! You are SPECIAL!!! ♡♥♡

JULY

7-1

PSALM 124:8 KJV *"Our help is in the Name of the Lord, Who made heaven and earth."*
Now as God made the heavens and earth (that was a very BIG project) and HE even takes care of the birds, etc. you need to realize HE will certainly take care of every one of your needs and desires. We call on HIS Name and HE supplies!!! ♡♥♡

7-2

JEREMIAH 32:27 KJV *"Behold, I AM the Lord, the God of all flesh: is there anything too hard for Me?"*
The answer is "NO" - absolutely nothing is too hard or too small for our God!!!! Trust Him. ♡♥♡
***Today is very special in the Brunt family - we always remember God's faithfulness to raise our son Cody from the dead and completely restore him from a drowning accident on July 2, 1997. Truly NOTHING is too hard for our GOD!

7-3

MARK 11:24 NLT *"I tell you, you can pray for anything, and if you believe that you've received it, it will be yours."*
Wishing doesn't work in the Kingdom of God. Praying according to God's Word does. When we pray, we believe we receive the answer. Be sure to read verse 23 and 24 together – they are foundation scriptures in prayer. *Gloria Copeland says "Prayer does not cause faith to work, faith causes prayer to work." ♡♥♡

7-4

HAPPY JULY 4th ☆★☆★

JOHN 15:5 MSG. *"However, apart from Me [cut off from vital union with Me] you can do nothing."*

As we celebrate our great nation's INDEPENDENCE DAY..... We should always be aware of our total DEPENDENCE on God. We really can't be truly successful without HIM. ☆★☆

7-5

HEBREWS 13:8 KJV *"Jesus Christ the same yesterday, today, and forever."*

HE never changes.... God IS love; He is faithful; He is all knowing...all good!!! You can count on HIM!! This is a power-packed verse, read it again. ♡♥♡

7-6

MATTHEW 6:33 AMP *"But seek (aim at and strive after) first of all His kingdom and His righteousness (His way of doing and being right), and then all these things taken together will be given you besides."*

When you put your Father God first priority in your life....HE will add to your life everything you need and more. It sounds too good to be true, but it *is* TRUE! ♡♥♡

7-7

MATTHEW 7:12 NKJV *"Therefore, whatever you want men to do to you, do also to them."*

You know this as THE GOLDEN RULE. This is definitely easier said than done. It's also like seeds sown...they bring forth the same kind...love→love; kindness→kindness, etc. Think before you speak or act to see if that is the way you would want someone to treat you. It will eventually come back to you. ♡♥♡

7-8

PSALM 141:2 NLT *"Accept my prayer as incense offered to You, and my upraised hands as an evening sacrifice."*
Every day we should pray and surrender our will, desires, thoughts, etc., to HIM. After all, HE knows us better than we know ourselves. HE sees the full picture of where we are and where HE desires for us to be. As we lift our hands to HIM, there is a physical release as well as a spiritual principle fulfilled that pleases HIM. ♡♥♡

7-9

ISAIAH 26:3 NKJV *"YOU will keep him in perfect peace, whose mind is stayed on YOU, because he trusts in YOU."*
The last part of the verse is why the first part works. Do you REALLY trust God to take care of you? Or do you try to fix it and when it doesn't work – you ask Him for help. Total trust and dependence on HIM is what HE desires. It's not a sign of weakness. It is TRUST. Then, the product of trust is the peace (total supply) of God. Money can't buy this peace! There is NOTHING like the peace of God. ♡♥♡

7-10

PROVERBS 18:24 KJV *"A man that hath friends must shew himself friendly: and there is a friend that sticketh closer than a brother."*
We all make friends in our lifetime. To have friends...you must be friendly to make them. The friends we surround ourselves with can encourage and build us up, or they can pull us down and slow our progress. It is very important that we surround ourselves with friends who speak God's Word and Will into our lives. Ultimately we have THE BEST FRIEND possible...in Jesus. HE is always there, HE will always have your back, front, sides, everything. What a FRIEND is HE!!!! ♡♥♡

7-11

1 CORINTHIANS 1:30 AMP *"But it is from Him that you have your life in Christ Jesus, whom God made our <u>Wisdom</u>.... "*
In-Christ <u>is</u> the place to be. Jesus has become our wisdom. He is in us, so wisdom has been deposited in us already, it is there for the times we need it. Do you need wisdom today? Wisdom is in you – ASK God to reveal it to you. ♡♥♡

7-12

EPHESIANS 1:13 NKJV *"In Him you also trusted, after you heard the word of truth, the gospel of your salvation...."*
The world needs to hear the "gospel" (the Good News), the story of Jesus' love. God is not trying to keep people at arm's-length. HE desires to be the loving Heavenly Father to all. Don't let this message of salvation be silent, spread the Word and be a part of sharing the Good News to the world. Someone shared this gospel with you - now you go share it with someone else. Keep the love flowing! ♡♥♡

7-13

ISAIAH 54:17 NKJV *"No weapon formed against you shall prosper...."*
This verse doesn't say there will never be things that will attack you. In life, oppositions DO come. What the verse says is that those things WILL NOT be successful against you. God ALWAYS will make wrongs right - as you stay with Him. God WILL be with you and bring you through. Stay close to Jesus!!! ♡♥♡

7-14

PROVERBS 3:24 NKJV "When you lie down, you will not be afraid; Yes, you will lie down and your sleep will be sweet."
There are few things that are more refreshing in life than a good night's sleep. God promises that our sleep would be sweet too. Claim it when you lay your head on your pillow and receive your sweet sleep! It sure beats counting sheep!!! ♡♥♡

7-15

PROVERBS 3:26 NKJV *"For the Lord will be your confidence...."*
In high school and college I had a confidence problem. I just felt so
insufficient and it hindered me from being and doing all God wanted
me to be and to do. This scripture really pulled me up and turned my
life around. That's what His "Rhema" word will do for you too.
Study His Word - it is life-food for you. ♡♥♡

7-16

PROVERBS 18:10 NLT *"The name of the Lord is a strong fortress; the
godly run to Him and are safe."*
I love this verse. There is a safe place in God!! God is the ONLY true
and living God. Just like our name reflects our character, God's name
shows the multiple facets of His character. I will spend the next week
looking at some of the names of God. Whatever your situation
is....HE has given us His Name that trumps anything that comes
against you. God is FOR YOU!! ♡♥♡

7-17

Names of God #1

ELOHIM - the God above all gods.

GENESES 1:1 KJV *"In the beginning God created the heaven and the
earth."*

NTB *"EL" generic word for God in the Semitic languages; name borrowed
by Hebrews from Canaanites, although they usually used plural form
Elohim."* pg. 247
I understand India has thousands of gods; other religions have all
kinds of statues they pray to, but our heavenly Father God is Elohim
- a living, caring, listening, personal God who loves us more than we
could ever comprehend. Think about that today. Our Elohim is the
only God who can create! HE is above all other gods because He IS
the only TRUE GOD that lives and loves us!! ♡♥♡

7-18

Names of God #2

JEHOVAH-JIREH – Jehovah will provide **NTB** p. 510; The Lord will see, or, provide.

GENESIS 22:14 KJV *"And Abraham called the name of that place Jehovah-jireh; as it is said to this day, In the mount of the Lord it shall be seen."*

It is good to remember how God has provided for you throughout your life. We immediately think of Abraham on top of the mountain - knife in hand, with his arm raised about to offer Isaac in obedience to God. Then the ram bleated out as it was caught in the bush. This is the first mention of Jehovah-Jireh in the Bible.

God' character as our Father God is to provide WHATEVER you need. That includes a lot of stuff...but that's how big our God is. Rest assured, He knows what you need better than you do, and He will take care of you!!! Be thankful! ♡♥♡

7-19

Names of God #3

EL-SHADDAI - the Almighty God **NTB** p. 251.

EXODUS 6:3 KJV *"And I appeared unto Abraham, unto Isaac, and unto Jacob, by the name of God Almighty, but by My name Jehovah was I not known to them."*

There is absolutely NOTHING our God cannot do. He made the universe, animals, rocks, plants, etc. Almighty is a limitless term. The only thing God Almighty cannot do is lie, which would contradict His Word. That's why it is so important to study His Word and know what is rightfully yours and trust Him for it. You can find rest in the Almighty God knowing that HE knows all about you, loves you and will take care of everything you need. Jesse Duplantis calls Him the "El Shad Dad." What a privilege to be His child! ♡♥♡

Ella C. Brunt

7-20

Names of God # 4

JEHOVAH-RAPHA – our Healer.

EXODUS 15:26 KJV *"...for I am the Lord that healeth thee."*

I've heard people call Jesus our "Great Physician," but doctors only treat symptoms; they cannot heal anyone. Our God IS THE HEALER!!!! He can actually create body parts that no longer work, or aren't there at all! As long as we are alive on this earth - we need to rely on our Jehovah-Rapha to keep us healthy and physically functioning to get His work done through us. ♡♥♡

7-21

Names of God #5

JEHOVAH-SHALOM – Jehovah is Peace.

JUDGES 6:24 JUB *"Then Gideon built an altar there* unto the Lord and called it The Lord is the Peace, {YHWH-shalom)...."*

The Jewish people greet each other with "Shalom" instead of "Hello" like we do. In doing so, they speak a blessing of peace on each other. Peace is not just a calm peaceful feeling. Peace in Hebrew is a state of being where all your needs are met, nothing missing or lacking. God's name today lets you know He not only has peace, but He IS peace. We need to have His peace not only in the tough times, but a state of peace should be where we dwell consistently. ♡♥♡

7-22

Names of God #6

JEHOVAH-SHAMMA – Jehovah is here.

EZEKIEL 48:35 JUB *"...and the name of the city from that day shall be, THE Lord IS HERE."*

One of the devil's tactics is to isolate you and have you think you are going through your situation all by yourself. But you are NEVER ALONE in any situation. Moses asked the name of God so he could tell the Israelites *Who* talked to him from the burning bush. God said "I AM" meaning I AM whatever you need; I AM ever present. The God Who is present is always with you!!!!! ♡♥♡

7-23

Names of God #7

YAHWEH – [Yhwh] our loving, covenant-keeping God.

NTB – *"the Hebrew name for God, known as tetragrammaton, four consonants, standing for ancient Hebrew name for God. Yahweh."* p. 1097

GENESIS 2:4 *"…in the day that the Lord God made the earth and the heavens."*

"Yhwh – His name was written without vowels, because it was never to be spoken aloud." (*The Names of God* by Lester Sumrall).

First of all God doesn't just have love…but HE IS LOVE. So everything HE is and does is consumed and motivated in love! Wow! It is soooooo very important to read, study, and know The Word because that is God's manual how He operates and His guidelines. In the Western culture, we don't understand just how important "covenant" is, but when you understand the unbreakable agreements God has put in force - you can always find the promise in the Bible, take it to the Father and He will fulfill that covenant. HE IS so faithful!! ♡♥♡

7-24

Names of God #8

JEHOVAH-NISSI – Jehovah is my banner

EXODUS 17:15 NKJV *"And Moses built an altar and called its name, The-Lord-Is-My-Banner."*

If you have ever played sports or been in competition of some kind, you know the importance of winning and accomplishing VICTORY - a great feeling for sure.

When we are in Christ, HE has already won our victories for us. You see, in Him…we are the victors!! In His name Jehovah-Nissi, we are victorious. This is not just a quality…it IS who HE is and who we are in Him. Whatever battle or trial you are in, declare Jehovah-Nissi - your victory has already been won; you just need to stay close to Jesus and depend on Him to carry you to the winning podium. ♡♥♡

7-25

EPHESIANS 1:21 KJV *"(Jesus is seated) far above all principality, and power, and might, and dominion, and every name that is named...."*
Jesus has been given a Name that supersedes all others! When you pray for people to be healed, it is important to use the Name of Jesus to dominate that illness or disease. Sicknesses have names – but the Name of Jesus is above any other name and has to bow!! Use the Name of Jesus to take dominion – just like He commanded Adam to do back in the garden (Gen. 1:26). ♡♥♡

7-26

COLOSSIANS 3:23 JNT *"Whatever work you do, put yourself into it, as those who are serving not merely other people, but the Lord."*
I have been reading in my Jewish New Testament...very interesting to study the Hebrew roots.
So as you go to your jobs and work, don't work for just a paycheck, but work as unto the Lord. HE will promote you, and give you positions you may not even be experienced in, but your attitude, excellence and His favor have rewards!!!! ♡♥♡

7-27

HEBREWS 12:15 JNT *"See to it that no one misses out on God's grace, that no ROOT OF BITTERNESS springing up causes trouble and thus contaminates many...."*
Life happens; life is not fair - but God is. Things happen to us that can cause us to be better or bitter. It is a choice you make. Don't let bitterness get a stronghold in your thinking. Keep your thoughts based on HIS Word, and then the fruit that comes out will be good fruit. God's grace will be what carries you through tough situations and His grace has sweet benefits! ♡♥♡

7-28

1 CORINTHIANS 1:25 NKJV *"Because the foolishness of God is wiser than men, and the weakness of God is stronger than men."*
The more we learn about our Heavenly Father God, we understand just how BIG, WISE, and LOVING He is. It is a never ending learning experience we have started here, but it will continue throughout eternity as we constantly learn new facets of God's character. God is so awesome!!!! And to think He truly loves us!!!! That should put a smile on your face today and last all day long. Just think about that!!!!
♡♥♡

7-29

1 JOHN 4:16 KJV *"And we have known and believed the love that God hath for us. GOD IS LOVE; and he that dwelleth in love dwelleth in God, and God in him."*
As the saying goes, "You become who you hang around with...." As you spend time fellowshipping with your Heavenly Father, His love grows in you and will be seen in your words and actions. ♡♥♡

7-30

PSALM 143:10A NLT *"Teach me to do Your will, for You are my God...."*
You never reach a place where there is nothing more to learn. Stay teachable...whether it is in your job or with the things of God. HE will give you wisdom and knowledge if you ask. Sometimes when we get to a place where we are "stuck" - HE knows just what to do, so just whisper "LORD help me," and HE hears and answers! HE is your God and he desires to lead and guide you! Nothing is too small or insignificant, so be totally dependent on Him. ♡♥♡

7-31

PROVERBS 11:3 AMP *"The <u>integrity</u> of the upright shall guide them, but the willful contrariness and crookedness of the treacherous shall destroy them."*

A simple definition of the word "integrity" is - doing the right thing even when nobody is looking. Of course we know Who is always looking over us and we may fool people around us, but we know the ultimate BOOKKEEPER! This verse basically deals with the seeds you sow....you will ultimately reap. It may not be easy to always DO the right thing, but it reaps great rewards. And just because it may look like someone "gets away with something," down the road...pay day will come. Be a person of integrity no matter what - it will lead you into better paths. ♡♥♡

AUGUST

8-1

ISAIAH 30:21 AMP *"And your ears will hear a word behind you, saying, This is the way, walk in it...."*
As children of the Most High God we communicate with Him on a spiritual level. We talk to Him in our language. Since our God IS a Spirit, HE communicates to us through our spirits. When we need guidance or instruction, HE will talk to us. Not to our heads...but to our hearts. Many times you may not understand with your head, but stay sensitive to your spirit and follow Him. HE will be that voice inside leading you in the right path. Of course we need spiritual ears to hear. Stay in close fellowship with Him and you will recognize His voice. ♡♥♡

8-2

ISAIAH 43:19 AMP *"Behold, I am doing a new thing!"*
Today is a brand new day. A day of opportunities, new adventures...things that you may be unfamiliar with and may be new to you. I want to challenge you today with two words or choices: BELIEVE or GRIEVE--sound like opposites don't they?
We spend much too much time regretting or looking in our past. Grief is sometimes a necessary stage, but don't get stuck there. Let the past go and stop grieving about what happened or what didn't happen that should have happened. Stop grieving and start BELIEVING God to bring you into a better place!!! HE is really good at that! Look away from your grief and trust and BELIEVE!!! ...You know I'm right. ♡♥♡

8-3

REVELATION 12:11 NLT *"And they have defeated him (satan) by the blood of the Lamb and by their testimony...."*

The second part of this verse is what I want to emphasize today. We are overcomers in Christ and we all have a testimony. All of us have gone through tough times/tests and have come out victoriously. Because we trust God, HE is our victory that brings us t-h-r-o-u-g-h. When we get on the other side of the test...He gives us the TESTimony we can share to encourage others. This is one aspect of "being blessed to be a blessing." Our testimony can and will help others know God's goodness will get them through tough times as well. We are God's walking, talking billboards!!!! ♡♥♡

8-4

PSALM 150:6 KJV *"Let everything that hath breath praise the Lord. Praise ye the Lord."*

Verse one of Ps.150 and the last verse make the statement, "Praise ye the Lord." Praise is the Hebrew word "Hallelujah," or "Praise You, JAH." The universal word in all languages is "Hallelujah" - praise. This is not a suggestion; it is a command – "You praise the Lord." No one can praise God for you, only you can. We might as well be practicing our praise here because it will continue throughout eternity. Praise brings victory. Praise brings you up emotionally. Praise brings you into the presence of God! HE sits enthroned in our praise. You want God to show up...praise Him and He will! Shout "Hallelujah" - a one-word praise and you will literally feel better! You praise and you will be raised to a higher level. If you are still breathing...praise the Lord!! ♡♥♡

8-5

PSALM 73:24 NLT *"You guide me with your counsel, leading me to a glorious destiny."*

God has a great plan, a purpose and a destiny for you! God has a reason for your existence at this time, this place for you. HE will guide you with His counsel (His Word).

(Continued on the next page)

(Continued from previous page)

As you give Him first place and first choice in everything you do, it will unfold into an amazing journey you could have never planned on your own. Your adventure in faith is like no other. You have a responsibility to do your part – spend time with Jesus and allow His Word to be your guide in everything you say and do. ♡♥♡

8-6

HEBREWS 8:10 AMP *"For this is the covenant that I will make.... I will imprint My laws upon their minds, even upon their innermost thoughts and understanding, and engrave them upon their hearts; and I will be their God, and they shall be My people;"*

God is really serious about His relationship with us. Look at the words "imprint" and "engrave." These are not temporary fixes. These actions are permanent, and He will permanently be our guide with His Word and Spirit! ♡♥♡

8-7

JOHN 4:41 AMP *"Then many more believed in and adhered to and relied on Him because of His personal message [what He Himself said]."*

We live in a time that we MUST have a personal relationship with Jesus. We can't get by with what others say, but we must spend time in prayer and in the Word to mature and develop to stay strong when "life situations" come. What is His personal message to you today? He has one for you - seek Him!! ♡♥♡

8-8

JAMES 5:16B AMP *"...The earnest (heartfelt, continued) prayer of a righteous man makes tremendous power available [dynamic in its working]."*

We need to be reminded just how much our prayers really are effective and powerful. Things change in the spiritual realm before they manifest in the physical. Know today that your prayers are actively bringing changes in you and situations you target them to. Prayer really does bring change! ♡♥♡

8-9

1 JOHN 1:9 AMP *"If we [freely] admit that we have sinned and confess our sins, He is faithful and just (true to His own nature and promises) and will forgive our sins [dismiss our lawlessness] and [continuously] cleanse us from all unrighteousness [everything not in conformity to His will in purpose, thought, and action]."*
John is writing to Believers in this book. I don't know any perfect people. Jesus--Who is our example--was the only perfect person. Jesus knows we will miss the mark and mess up; it certainly doesn't take HIM by surprise. I'm so thankful for this verse that lets me know when I do miss it – I can come to HIM, confess it, receive HIS forgiveness and continue moving forward. Don't get down on yourself when you miss it. God knew we would sin, but He lets us know that IF we confess those sins, that we already have been forgiven and can stand in HIS righteousness. What a deal! Don't go around bummed out because you missed it in some area, just be quick to run to Him, and confess it. He SO loves us and cleanses us from ALL sin. ♡♥♡

8-10

PSALM 3:3 AMP *"But You, O Lord, are a shield for me, my glory and the lifter of my head."*
David was in trouble, but he knew his God. He trusted in God. David believed God to—
  - protect him (shield);
  - to give him strength and the very presence of God (glory) to be with him;
  - to encourage him (lift up his head) and give him the confidence – (no more shame or inferiority) - he so needed to continue on and not quit.

Look at how God came through as David relied on the Lord to do what he couldn't do in himself. You can ALWAYS count on Jesus to get you t-h-r-o-u-g-h!! ♡♥♡

8-11

PROVERBS 17:17 NKJV *"A friend loves at all times, and a brother is born for adversity."*
We will meet a lot of people along our life's journey. Some will be acquaintances that will come in and out of our lives for a short time. Others will come in our lives and remain like family - brothers and sisters. These will help us through adversities and the tough times. God knows who to bring to you at the right time and for the right season. Our part is to be a good friend and love with His love. Be a blessing to someone today. ♡♥♡

8-12

PSALM 147:3 NKJV *"He heals the brokenhearted and binds up their wounds."*
In life "stuff" happens. We get hurt inside, where no one sees but God. Our emotions and feelings get ripped apart...but God binds those unseen wounds with His love and they begin to mend. It IS a process that takes time, but when we get to the other side, the healing is so complete that the wound is only a faint memory. No one can touch you like Jesus can! ♡♥♡

8-13

MARK 10:27 NKJV *"But Jesus looked at them and said, 'With men it is impossible, but not with God; for with God all things are possible'."*
Even though His disciples were totally confused by what Jesus was teaching on in the previous verses...HE knew just how to get their attention. Regardless of how impossible your situation may seem to you--take note and remember this verse. ALL means "all"-- and God's got you and all that you are facing taken care of. You are in good hands with Jesus! ♡♥♡

8-14

DANIEL 5:12 KJV *"Because an excellent spirit, knowledge and understanding...."*
The Bible says of Daniel, that "an excellent spirit was in him...." At your job, home, wherever you are and whatever you do - do it with excellence. The Lord is recording the work of your hands. HE is the God of Excellence! Believers should be the best employees since you do not work as unto men - but to God. Even when no one is around, always work as if the Lord is right there with you, because HE is!!! ♡♥♡

8-15

II PETER 3:9 KJV *"For the Lord is not slack concerning His promise...."*
Are you believing God for something based in His Word? If you are, and if you have a scripture you are standing on - it will come to pass. HE may be preparing you for it, but you can count on Him to fulfill His promise to you. ♡♥♡

8-16

EZEKIEL 22:30 NKJV *"So I sought for a man among them who would make a wall, and stand in the gap before Me on behalf of the land, that I should not destroy it; but I found no one."*
So many times we pray for ourselves which is good, but we should also daily pray for our nation and leaders as well as for Israel and its leaders. God's blessings are on us to bless others and prayer is one way we "stand in the gap." These are prophecy-fulfilling days and both nations need our prayer support. In doing so, we are blessed by our obedience to hold them up in prayer. ♡♥♡

Ella C. Brunt

8-17

EPHESIANS 2:10 KJV *"For we are His workmanship, created in Christ Jesus unto good works, which God hath before ordained that we should walk in them."*

Did you realize you are a piece of WORK!!! Yep, when you chose Jesus as your Lord, He made you a brand new person. Also the verse says we are created to do good works. God has a path and purpose He desires for us to walk in and work well ~ as we live our lives through Him. Your life is exciting and full of great things your Father has prepared for you. Enjoy!!! ♡♥♡

8-18

ROMANS 14:12 NKJV *"So then each of us shall give account of himself to God."*

I like to say it like this - God is the Bookkeeper. All you are responsible for and are able to control is YOU. When someone treats you wrong, it hurts. But in the end, the Lord sees it and they will give an account of it to HIM. It may even seem that they get by with it...but not so. We will all stand before the Lord and give an account of our actions and thoughts. I don't know about you, but that's about all I can handle, just to keep myself straight. You are not in control of others, so just do your best and keep going. ♡♥♡

8-19

I KINGS 8:27B NKJV *"...Behold, heaven and the heaven of heavens cannot contain You...."*

King Solomon had just finished building an elaborate temple for God. He was in awe of God's glory and presence coming and filling the temple at the dedication service. This prayer shows just how BIG our God is. You can never fit Him in a "box." His ways are much higher and better than you could ever imagine. Our Heavenly Father knows you, knows you better than you know yourself.

(Continued on the next page)

79

(Continued from previous page)
HE is looking out for you and loves you more than you can possibly comprehend. There is nothing He can't do! Our God is awesome! And best of all He chose us to place His Spirit in 24/7. He dwells in us! How wonderful is that!! ♡♥♡

8-20

JOHN 21:25 NKJV *"And there are also many other things that Jesus did, which if they were written one by one, I suppose that even the world itself could not contain the books that would be written. Amen."*
This last sentence John closed his book with lets us know the story of Jesus continues. He always has been and forever will be. All the books about Jesus have not been written and if they were written, the world could not contain them. It's hard to wrap your brain about that one for sure. But in reality, you have a book that could be written about your life's story. The hand of God IS on your life and you have a story of God's keeping and protecting power. You are special to Him!! ♡♥♡

8-21

JAMES 1:19 KJV *"Wherefore, my beloved brethren, let every man be swift to hear, slow to speak, slow to wrath;"*
Pastor James of the church at Jerusalem was giving some good advice to his congregation of qualities to have in times of trials.
1 - First of all, we need to hear the whole story. Every story has two
     sides (or more). Get your facts straight.
2 – Secondly, be slow to comment to others. We all like to put in our
     own opinion don't we? Just hold that and know that when you do
     speak, your words can be life or death to situations.
3 – Third, be slow to get angry. Short tempers usually don't benefit
     people. Be patient and make sure if and when you do act or
     speak that it is in kindness, self-control, and brings honor to God.
These are three very good traits to have at any time, not just during tough situations. ♡♥♡

Ella C. Brunt

8-22

PROVERBS 11:25 NKJV *"The generous soul will be made rich, and he who waters will also be watered himself."*

This is another example of sowing and reaping. Everything you say and do are "seeds." The words you speak are powerful and they have creative power – in the positive or negative – you choose. If you are a generous person, God will make sure your every need is met because you are giving out to bless others.

If you are stingy with your actions toward others, other people will not be giving into your life either. The sowing/reaping principle is far-reaching and will always work in your life. We just have to make sure we are sowing good seeds in order to reap a good harvest. ♡♥♡

8-23

EPHESIANS 4:32 KJV *"And be ye kind one to another, tenderhearted, forgiving one another, even as God for Christ's sake hath forgiven you."*

Now that is a powerful Word. This is not a suggestion, but a command. This is an attribute He desires us to BE - not just occasionally use, but to BE. We can be kind in our words and actions BEcause God has forgiven us through what Jesus did on the cross. We have HIS ability to BE kind. "Kind" means good, gracious and easy. Maybe in ourselves it would be hard to pull this off...but BEcause of Jesus and His ability in us, we can BE! It's not so much who you are, it is who you BE. ♡♥♡

8-24

PROVERBS 3:13, 16 KJV *"Happy is the man who finds wisdom.... Length of days is in her right hand; and in her left hand riches and honour."*

When we GET wisdom, it brings longevity, riches, and honor. You see! Star Trek didn't coin the phrase "Live long and prosper" – God did!!! Wisdom is found in God's Word. Wisdom is the correct application of knowledge. You have to go after wisdom – get it! What you seek after is what you will get. Wisdom is like a treasure. (Continued on the next page)

81

(Continued from previous page)

You seek it, dig it out, and you will find and possess it. It is a life-long process. There is always more to know. Be a life-long learner. Get wisdom – then you will live long and prosper!! ♡♥♡

8-25

GENESIS 6:22 NKJV *"Thus Noah did; according to all that God commanded him, so he did."*

I want the Lord to say those words to me – "Ella did, according to all that God commanded her, so she did." I want the Lord to say those words to you as well. To walk in obedience to the Lord for all He asked us to do. "ObeDIEnce" is a powerful word and in the middle is the word "die." We will have to "die" to ourselves in order to live the life God wants us to live. I'm sure Noah questioned in his mind the practicality of the ark plans. No one had ever seen rain before, so how was all this water supposed to come and make this big boat float? We may not see what God is doing in our lives, but as we walk in obedience to him, we will see how good His plan is. Stay close to Jesus and listen to His voice – He will never give you bad advice. ♡♥♡

8-26

PSALM 115:8 NKJV *"Those who make them (idols) are like them; so is everyone who trusts in them."*

Idols are not just wooden, silver, gold, etc. figures people worship. Many worship – give their love and attention -- to many THINGS/idols. We need to be very aware of any THING that may get to be a higher priority than the Lord Himself. If we could get to a point in our lives where Jesus is and remains first place – HE will take care of every need we could possibly have. It sounds easy, but it isn't. So many voices and distractions that pull on our time and attention want to take that first place position! Remember, all these other things are temporal and will pass away all too fast. Just like humans make and form idols, this scripture says that these people become dead just like the idol.

(Continued on the next page)

(Continued from previous page)

The idol is dead and anyone who trusts in the idols brings death into their lives. As humans, we have the choice to make sure no idol will have priority as the center of our love and take the place that God wants for Himself. If you trust in those idols, you become like them – spiritually dead. This is heavy stuff, but many are trapped in that reality. Keep Jesus first priority!! ♡♥♡

8-27

MATTHEW 7:7 NKJV *"Ask, and it will be given to you; seek and you will find; knock, and it will be opened to you."*

I like to put this as an acronym – A-S-K – Ask, Seek, Knock. Salvation is a free gift from God, but when we become a part of the Family of God – there are some requirements we need to fulfill to receive all that God has for us. I could put $10,000 in your bank account, but if you don't realize it's there, or you never make withdrawals, it will remain in there and be of no benefit. Jesus has completed the work God had Him perform for everything we would ever need. It is up to us to ASK according to the Word; SEEK Him and use the Word to know what we have in Him; KNOCK and gain access to everything that has been deposited in our accounts. God is not trying to withhold things from you! He wants you to gain access to everything He has for you. Asking for things is the easy part – being responsible for it is the part that develops character. ♡♥♡

8-28

LUKE 7:23 NKJV *"And blessed is he who is not offended because of Me."*

In our days of 'political correctness' people are getting in trouble for just saying, "God bless you," when someone in the room sneezes. Too many people are "offended" any time the reference to God and especially the name of Jesus is spoken any place other than the church house. It seems like Christians are under attack from people who are "intolerant" to those who don't think and believe like they do, but expect Christians to be tolerant of anything that is ungodly. (Continued on the next page)

(Continued from previous page)

The scripture says we are blessed when we are not offended because of Jesus. (Jesus said this verse -- it is in red letters). Christians have many blessings listed in the Bible and this is a promise you can count on. Are you ashamed of Jesus? You have a blessing waiting on you as you show honor to Jesus wherever you are – in church or in public. You will be blessed if you are not offended because of Him. ♡♥♡

8-29

DEUTERONOMY 7:6 NKJV *"For you are a holy people to the Lord God; the Lord your God has chosen you to be a people for Himself, a* special treasure *above all peoples on the face of the earth."*

When you became "born again," you became a member of the family of God. I know in the New Testament, you are called a "chosen generation," but I like this verse in the Old Testament that calls us a "special treasure" to God. Do you know and realize just how "special" you are to Him? The Almighty God, Creator of the universe calls you such a tender pet name. Any time you have a bad day, just think about God's pet name for you. You are a "special treasure" to God; you are like the "teacher's pet" – HE has special privileges for you to enjoy!! ♡♥♡

8-30

PROVERBS 1:33 NKJV *"But whoever listens to me will dwell safely, and will be secure, without fear of evil."*

We are living in a very violent society. Road rage, violent crimes, and acts of terrorism seem to be the lead stories on the evening newscasts. If you watch and listen to these evil reports, eventually you will have fear implanted in you. It would be easy to be fearful of getting out of the house.   BUT GOD has given His Word that if we listen to Him (study His Word, pray and hear His instructions) that we would live in safety. We can be free from fear and live in the peace of God; living in His security and without fear. Now that is a great place to live.   (Continued on the next page)

(Continued from previous page)

He gives us a promise but He also gives us a requirement – to listen to Him. Make sure you spend time with Jesus – our Great Shepherd – we will hear His voice because we are His sheep and His sheep hear His voice!!! The more time you spend with Him, the easier it is to hear His voice. ♡♥♡

8-31

COLOSSIANS 3:23 NKJV *"And whatsoever you do, do it heartily, as unto the Lord and not to men."*

This verse will definitely keep our lives in perspective. Always keep the mindset of God, Who is the ultimate "Bookkeeper" and whatever your career or job may be, realize that HE is the one you answer to. Whether we are at home or working for someone else, we should have a "spirit of excellence" in our productivity as well as attitude. Don't do just enough to get by, but do more than enough -- go above what is required. Your life is to represent the kingdom of God and people will take notice and see Jesus in the way you act and react. Whatever you do, do it with a good attitude and with excellence. ♡♥♡

SEPTEMBER

9-1

ECCLESIASTES 7:12 KJV *"For wisdom is a defense, and money is a defense: but the excellence of knowledge is, that wisdom giveth life to them that have it."*

You have heard the story – "If you give a man a fish, he eats for the day, but if you teach him to fish, he will have food for a lifetime." Wisdom is the key ingredient in life. You can have all the knowledge in the world, but not know how to accurately apply that knowledge…it is not beneficial. True wisdom is the correct application of knowledge. Wisdom is something we can "get" (Proverbs 4:5). Jesus has been made unto us wisdom (I Corinthians 1:30). Wisdom is not a "carrot" the Lord dangles in front of us that is unobtainable; HE has <u>given</u> us His wisdom. It resides in us, but we have to develop it. We ask for wisdom and do our part. He promised to give wisdom to us. Wisdom is the principle thing so get it! ♡♥♡

9-2

MATTHEW 15:8 NLT *"These people honor Me with their lips, but their heart is far from Me."*

Jesus is teaching the scribes and Pharisees and quoted this verse from Isaiah 29:13. We can go to church and go through all the motions of singing praise and worship, listening and "amen-ing" the sermon as the minister preaches, but in all that action – our hearts aren't in it. We can go to church and participate, doing everything with our heads and not out of a <u>heart</u> devotion to the Lord. How it grieves the heart of God when we really don't mean what we say and do to honor Him. HE deserves first place in everything we do to. Let's love Him with our whole heart! ♡♥♡

9-3

PSALM 34:7 NKJV *"The angel of the Lord encamps all around those who fear Him, and delivers them."*

It is very comforting to know we are never alone. Jesus is always with us; the Holy Spirit lives inside us. We even have God's angels positioned around us! The "catch" is IF we fear (worship) Him. To fear the Lord is not to be afraid of Him, but to love, honor, respect, and worship Him. When you really love someone, you want to give your love and attention to them. When you love the Lord, you want to please Him and give Him your attention and time. As you love (fear) the Lord, He has promised to protect and deliver you. ♡♥♡

9-4

3 JOHN 2 NKJV *"Beloved, I pray that you may prosper in all things and be in health, just as your soul prospers."*

I agree with John today and believe God to bless (empower you) in everything you do today so you will be healthy in your mind, spirit and body. This verse is very endearing and sincere. The King James version of this verse says "I wish above all things...", but I like the New King James version much better. I'd much rather have someone pray for me than wish for me wouldn't you? The prosperity and health are yours, just as much as how our soul (mind, will and emotions) are sound and stable. It is so very important for your soul to be at peace, stable and consistent. When your soul prospers, it gives God full permission to bless you with prosperity and health. For such a short scripture, it sure is full of power to the Believer. ♡♥♡

9-5

ISAIAH 41:10 NKJV *"Fear not, for I AM with you; Be not dismayed, for I AM your God. I will strengthen you, Yes, I will help you, I will uphold you with My righteous right hand."*

(Continued on the next page)

(Continued from previous page)

We know that fear is a terrible emotion. Joyce Meyer has the acronym the word "fear" - F-false E-evidence A-appearing R-real. Too many times we feel fear and it is because of something that isn't even there.

You have to remind yourself that the devil IS DEFEATED, so he just lies about having any power over you. God tells us in this verse to NOT FEAR because HE is with us – now that is a comforting promise! He goes on to say don't worry because He is your God. (Humanists are their own god; numerous religions worship many false gods). Settle the issue! God Almighty is <u>your</u> God. Then as we do that, His agreement is to help us and hold us up by His right hand (indicates strength). God will help and strengthen you. God really is on your side and desires to protect you and keep you safe.♡♥♡

9-6

REVELATION 1:3 NKJV *"<u>Blessed</u> is he who <u>reads</u> and those who <u>hear</u> the words of this prophecy, and <u>keep</u> those things which are written in it; for the time is near."*

What a timely scripture! We are living in the last of the Last Days according to the Bible. This verse is in the last book of the Bible, and holds a promise to those who <u>read</u> and study the prophecies in the book of Revelation. The scripture could hold true for every chapter. If you want the wisdom of God, read and study His Word. This promise is specific to those who read the book of Revelation – <u>hear</u> and <u>do</u> what you read. The book of Revelation requires intense study. What John saw was not easy to put into descriptive words. What John saw was light years ahead of anything that was in his time (90-95 A.D.). You won't understand it the first time you read through this book! Keep on reading and rely on the Holy Spirit to enlighten you. One thing about it, it isn't wasted time and it carries a blessing with it. ♡♥♡

9-7

GENESIS 11:31 NKJV *"And Terah took his son Abram and his grandson Lot, the son of Haran, and his daughter-in-law Sarai, his son Abram's wife, and they went out with them from Ur of the Chaldeans to go to the land of Canaan; and they came to Haran and dwelt there."*

We hear a lot about Abram (later named Abraham—the Father of Faith) but not much about his father. In this verse, Abram's father Terah left his family and brought three people with him to go to Canaan. He never made it to Canaan, but settled in Haran. When God gives you instructions to do something, HE desires obedience. This verse lets us know Terah started something but did not finish it. In the next chapter we read how God spoke to Abram to leave Haran and go where HE would instruct him. This was a harder request to obey! Notice that God did not give Abram a specific destination. Many times the Lord will give us instruction, but not the whole plan. That's when we follow the Lord one step at a time and HE will show us the next step as we take the first step. Faith is like that – trusting God one step at a time and eventually the whole plan is revealed-- but you are well on your way to accomplish it. Who said faith is not an adventure? "Trust God" is a short phrase but very powerful. The benefits of doing so are absolutely limitless. ♡♥♡

9-8

LUKE 18:16 NKJV *"But Jesus called them to Him and said, "Let the little children come to Me, and do not forbid them; for of such is the kingdom of God."*

When Jesus taught, He used common language. You didn't need to reach a certain intellectual level to understand Him. Jesus had a personality that drew people to Him. It was common for Jesus to be surrounded by children (I think He was a fun person to be around and they saw that). Children learn so much in the first 5-6 years of their lives. Many foundations are laid in that time period.
(Continue on the next page)

(Continued from previous page)

The Gospel of Jesus seems so simple, yet it is so profound - that as you are trusting as a child, the kingdom of God (which is righteousness, peace and joy) is available to us according to this verse. Too many times we complicate matters with the "what if's" in life. Jesus wants us to trust Him, just like children trust those who are overseeing them. We may not understand everything, but as we walk in step-by-step obedience to what He instructs us to do, we can know that He will continue to lead and direct us. The first step is to <u>come</u> to Him, spend time with Him in prayer and reading His Word, and simply "hang out" with Him. ♡♥♡

9-9

EPHESIANS 2:14 KJV *"For He is our peace, who hath made both one, and hath broken down the middle wall of partition (division) between us."*

There is nothing as important as having the peace of God in our lives. The word peace – Shalom -- means "nothing missing, nothing broken." The peace of God supplies us with whatever we need, when we need it. Jesus IS our peace and we can go directly to Him with any need we may have. Jesus paid the price on the cross for us and the veil that divided the people from the inner court or Holy of Holies was torn from top to bottom. <u>God Himself</u> tore the divider and for the first time ordinary people can go directly to God and talk to Him personally. God's peace is available to us 24/7. He delights in us coming to Him and spending time with Him. He IS our peace!!!! ♡♥♡

9-10

I JOHN 5:14 NKJV *"Now this is the confidence that we have in Him, that if we ask anything according to His will, He hears us."*

This is such a powerful verse. There was a time in my life that I felt very inferior. My self-confidence was so low, I felt uncomfortable just being around people. BUT GOD delivered me from that by His love and His Word. This verse is a cornerstone to give us the confidence to go to Him in prayer. (Continued on the next page)

(Continued from previous page)

It is also a declaration that we can search His Word and find scriptures/promises proving that what He did for people in the Bible, He WILL do that for us today. I like to pray the Word. If we ask anything according to His will – His will is His Word. In many older Bibles, the first page states "The Will and Testament of Our Lord." The Word of God gives us rights and privileges. This Word shows us—His children--what is available to us. Paul writes about "The riches of our inheritance." If you ever wonder if God hears your prayers - just pray His Will which is His Word! If you can find scripture for it – He wants us to have it! All we have to do is ask. ♡♥♡

9-11

ISAIAH 30:21 NKJV *"Your ears will hear a word behind you, saying, 'This is the way, walk in it,' whenever you turn to the right hand or whenever you turn to the left."*

This is a comforting verse that lets us know that the Lord desires to guide us. It is His desire to help us from going down the wrong path or get on the wrong plan. Unfortunately, sometimes we just aren't listening. Since Jesus came and gave us the Holy Spirit as our Guide, we have the ability to hear His directions and plans for our lives. We are not left on our own to barely get by. Stay close to Jesus and be sensitive to His leading to know exactly what you are to do and say, and where you are to go. Don't be deceived or receive wrong information. Humility is the protection against deception. Stay humble, teachable and listen to His voice and "your ears will hear...." You will have His Divine Guidance. ♡♥♡

9-12

JEREMIAH 29:11 NKJV *"For I know the thoughts that I think towards you, says the Lord, thoughts of peace and not of evil, to give you a future and a hope."*

You are in God's thoughts!!! How amazing that He thinks about us! We are on His mind! Not only is He thinking about you, but He has a great plan for your life and desires to give you a future that is full of peace. (Continued on the next page)

(Continued from previous page)
God is so amazing that He knows each of us by name and He has a plan and purpose for your life greater than you can even imagine. His plan is "NOT of evil" – His plan is full of peace. We have a Good God! ♡♥♡

9-13

JEREMIAH 29:12, 13 NKJV *"Then you will call upon Me and go and pray to Me, and I will listen to you. And you will seek Me and find Me, when you search for Me with all your heart."*
God is not trying to keep anything He has promised away from us. He is not playing "hide-n-go-seek" with us. When you take the time to talk with God (we call this prayer), He said He would listen to you. God is not too busy to hear you and listen to you. He desires that we seek Him and give Him first place – all of our heart. Whatever you need today, take this scripture with you in prayer and remind the Lord what He said in His Word. He loves for us to remind Him of what He has said and He will back it up every time! (Look at yesterday's verse that precedes this. If a verse begins with "therefore," "because," or like today's "then" – it's always good to go back to the previous verse or two and see just what that conjunction is "there for.") ♡♥♡

9-14

ROMANS 14:12 KJV *"So then each of us shall give account of himself to God."*
We really cannot live any way we want. There will be a day we will stand before God and give an account of how we lived our lives. Did we live our lives for ourselves, for our family, for our spouse, for our church, for what we thought others wanted us to do??? The list goes on, but the bottom line is that God IS the Bookkeeper and He will show us how we missed it, or how we hit the mark and accomplished what we were supposed to do. Quite a sobering thought. The way to be confident in the way we live is to constantly ask ourselves, "What is my motive?"
(Continued on the next page)

(Continued from previous page)
Are we doing what we do to look good, please other people – or to please God? We should constantly evaluate what we say and do and keep our motives pure. ♡♥♡

9-15

EPHESIANS 6:10 KJV *"Finally, my brethren, be strong in the Lord, and in the power of His might."*
Paul is closing out his letter by encouraging the Believers to "be strong." Notice he did not say to just "be strong" with your own strength, but with <u>His</u> might. I like to say it like this – do what you can do and then trust God to do what you can't do in your own ability. In life, we will always come across things that we can't do in our own abilities. When we get to those, be the first to ask God for help and rely on His might. Really--it's a good thing to lean on Him in everything we do so He gets all the credit anyway.
One thing you don't want to do is to make a plan and then ask God to bless it. Ask Him first for His Plan and it will already be blessed. ♡♥♡

9-16

PROVERBS 9:11 NKJV *"For by me your days will be <u>multiplied</u>, and years of life will be <u>added</u> to you."*
The ninth chapter of Proverbs deals with wisdom and understanding. Wisdom is the appropriate application of knowledge. As we are obedient to the Word of God, one of the benefits we receive is long life. In oriental cultures it is considered an honor to live long and the elderly citizens are highly respected and hold a prestigious position. Wisdom should be the natural result of a long life, especially for the children of God. The Bible promises us in Psalm 91:16, "With long life will I satisfy you." The fourth Commandment says, "Honor your father and mother, that your days may be long upon the land which the Lord your God is giving you" (Exodus 20:12). I like God's math better than ours!!! When <u>He</u> adds and multiplies, He takes us to a whole different realm! ♡♥♡

9-17

COLOSSIANS 3:17 NKJV *"And whatever you do in word or deed, do all in the name of the Lord Jesus, giving* thanks to God the Father through Him."

This is a verse that can be a measuring stick as far as what you say and do. Can you say what you want to say in Jesus' Name? Can you act out what want you what to do in Jesus' Name? If not, just don't say it or do it. Is it kind? Is it lovely? Is it good? The last part of the verse is giving thanks to God through Jesus. So, can you do it or say it in the Name of Jesus and then give thanks to God about it? This will certainly limit what we say or do doesn't it? ♡♥♡

9-18

THESSALONIANS 4:18 KJV *"Wherefore comfort one another with these words."*

Paul gives us some previous verses describing the Rapture of the Church -- when Jesus appears in the clouds and we rise up to meet Him. If you have ever had a loved one depart from this earth and go to heaven, these are comforting words to remind us that we will be re-united again.

This verse reminds us to comfort each other with these words – Jesus is coming back for us and He is also going to raise those loved ones up. We will be together with Him in the air! This is an event that is soon to be fulfilled. What a comfort it brings! Be ready! ♡♥♡

9-19

ROMANS 8:11 NKJV *"But if the Spirit of Him who raised Jesus from the dead dwells in you, He who raised Christ from the dead will also give life to your mortal bodies through His Spirit who dwells in you."*

"If" is signaling a choice here – if you have made Jesus the Lord of your life – then the Spirit of God lives in you! (Lower case "s" in the word "spirit" refers to your human spirit; Capital "S" in the word Spirit always refers to the Holy Spirit of God.) What an honor to have the Creator of the Universe living in us! The same power that raised Jesus from the dead resides IN US and makes alive (quickens) our mortal bodies. (Continued on the next page)

(Continued from previous page)
It is God's power that raised Jesus from the dead and HE is available to us to heal, strengthen, and restore our bodies to the perfection they were created to be. Don't settle for anything less than the best God has already provided for you – spirit, soul and body – the total price has been paid. You make the choice to draw on His power that is at work in you today. ♡♥♡

9-20

PSALM 57:7 NKJV *"My heart is steadfast, O God, my heart is steadfast; I will sing and give praise."*
Your "heart" is your soul/emotions (thoughts, feelings). The psalmist declared that his heart was steadfast. His emotions were steady and calm even in the time of problems. We will always have a choice to either cave in to the problems we face – or with God's strength and our relationship with Jesus – we will choose to be strong and not let the problems shake us up. This is not an easy thing to do. The last part gives us the key – to sing and give thanks to God. As you stay close to Jesus, HE will be your stability, HE will keep you calm, cool and collected even in the times of distress. Keep steady emotions and a song in your heart!!! ♡♥♡

9-21

LUKE 10:19 NKJV *"Behold, I give you authority to trample on serpents and scorpions, and over <u>all</u> the power of the enemy, and nothing shall by any means hurt you."*
Jesus is addressing the 70 that He had sent out to evangelize. They came back so excited about the miracles they experienced using the Name of Jesus. Jesus repeats part of His commission of Mark 16:17, 18. God has already given us authority to use the Name of Jesus. Don't blame God when things don't work out the way you want them to. Jesus gave us authority to defeat ALL satan's attacks and come out victorious. Jesus gets blamed for too many failures when He has never failed at all! Jesus FINISHED the work on the cross, paid the debt to give us back all Adam lost in The Fall.
(Continued on the next page)

(Continued from previous page)
Just like the 70, Jesus expects us to go and take authority over our sphere of influence using His Name. You go and DO and see His results! ♡♥♡

9-22

GALATIANS 6:9 NKJV *"And let us not grow weary while doing good, for in due season we shall reap if we do not lose heart."*
Paul encourages the early church to hang in there and not give up just because they didn't see things happening. As always, God sees your good works and records your deeds. His timing is always right. As Christians, our integrity is on display whether others see it or not. But God always sees! The Biblical principle of sowing and reaping is referred to in this verse. What you sow – you will eventually reap (verse 7 also) – that is a law of nature as well as a spiritual law. So if you are a little tired today and feel like all your hard work is not taking you anywhere – don't believe it – you will come out on top – just don't give up!!! ♡♥♡

9-23

MATTHEW 24:35 NKJV *"Heaven and earth will pass away, but My words will by no means pass away."*
Jesus is addressing the disciples on end-time events, and after the fig tree parable, He makes this profound statement. You need to keep in mind that your Bible is God's love letter and instruction to you. Jesus IS the Word! God spoke words to create the vast universe and best of all, we are made in His image. It is mind-boggling to realize we have His ability to speak His Word and share the power of His Word to enjoy His results. This promise gives us the unending power of His Word. There is coming a new heaven and new earth after the Millennium - He says that's going to happen – but His Words will never pass away. God's Word will not change. He says what He means and He means what He says. You will find His promises in the Bible. God will honor His Word; it's His promise to us. He cannot lie! (Continued on the next page)

97

(Continued from previous page)

It is so very important we study and read His Word daily because He will speak to us, instruct us and guide our steps as we let this living Word be first place in our lives.

It is never wasted time to read and study the Word of God. He will reveal His purposes for you through His Word. Use it as your standard, and you will walk in His Will. ♡♥♡

9-24

PROVERBS 19:20, 27 NKJV *"Listen to counsel and receive instruction, that you may be wise in your latter days…. Cease listening to instruction, my son, and you will stray from the words of knowledge."*

Solomon was a very wise man and he knew there was always more to learn. Godly wisdom is the principle thing to obtain. We should all be "Life-long learners." Large companies have "think tanks" where they are constantly looking at situations from different perspectives to see improved ways of doing things. Apart from the Word of God – which is the counsel of God – we get off track, so keep the Word as the center point. Listen and pay attention to wise counsel based on the Word. Search His Word for the instruction you need. Treasures aren't just sitting on top of the surface all the time; sometimes you need to make time to "dig" a little to uncover His instruction and "words of knowledge." God wants to share instructions with you from His Word, so give Him your time and attention. God is always speaking through His Word! Are you listening? ♡♥♡

9-25

EXODUS 15:26 NKJV *"If you diligently heed the voice of the Lord your God and do what is right in His sight, give ear to His commandments and keep all His statutes, I will put none of the diseases on you which I have brought on the Egyptians For I am the Lord who heals you."*

Jehovah Rapha is The God Who Heals You.

The children of Israel took 40 years to get Egypt out of them even though they were out of Egypt. God gave them an ordinance to follow (listen to God's voice, do the right thing, listen and keep true to The Word). HE promised to heal them. God didn't say they would never get sick, but if and when they did – HE would heal them. As this scripture says – since the Egyptians went against God, so the natural consequences of disobedience left the door open for diseases to come to them. (Keep in mind the Old Testament scriptures were under the Mosaic Covenant, the Law, but I believe we can claim His Promises in the entire Bible. When you are studying scriptures, always be aware of the time period and who the audience consists of.) God doesn't have diseases to hand out for sure. Jesus is in the healing business today. Many blessings are conditional –"IF" you do this, THEN God will do that. This passage lets us know the goodness of God. We have a Good, Faithful and Healing God! ♡♥♡

9-26

PROVERBS 10:7 KJV *"The memory of the just is blessed...."*

When my children were in school, I reminded them if they would study and put the information in their minds, then they could ask the Lord to bring that recall back when they had exams. I confess this verse over my mind for myself! I will not lose my mind to any disease – this scripture was true for Solomon and I claim it today. Believe for a healthy, sharp, alert, creative mind that serves you well all the days of your life. ♡♥♡

9-27

PSALM 89:18 KJV *"For the Lord is our defense; and the Holy One of Israel is our king."*

This verse will encourage you today. Sometimes we are placed in situations that look impossible to recover from or get out of. Jesus is at work giving us His Favor to reign over those impossible situations and make a way out that only HE can. We have to keep a grip on our emotions – NEVER let your emotions rule over you! Let your spirit rule over your soul (mind, will and emotions). Know in your heart that God is working on your behalf, working behind the scenes to bring you through on HIS path. Don't carry around things you have no control over – let Him take that responsibility. He's very good at making wrong things right! ♡♥♡

9-28

EPHESIANS 1:15, 16 KJV *"Therefore I also, after I heard of your faith in the Lord Jesus and your love for all the saints, do not cease to give thanks for you, making mention of you in my prayers."*

The next verses 17-23 go on to record what Paul actually prayed for his new friends in the faith. These are great scriptures to pray for specific things you are believing for - not only others, but you can also pray them over yourself. We need to pray specifically over our family, friends, neighbors, government, military, etc. When you do, it is easy to make a check-off list as God answers those prayers. Start your prayer diary today if you haven't already. ♡♥♡

9-29

HEBREWS 10:12 KJV *"But this Man, after He had offered one sacrifice for sins forever, sat down at the right hand of God."*
The book of Hebrews goes into a lot detail comparing the Old Testament tabernacle and Law to show how Jesus came and completely fulfilled every requirement. The tabernacle had NO seat for the priests to sit in because their work was never finished. Jesus however, came and fulfilled The Law and offered His own blood as our sacrifice. Then He <u>sat down</u> at God's right hand signifying all the work was done. So, that means Jesus has done His part – now we are to go and do our part. Live a victorious, blessed, overcoming life! ♡♥♡

9-30

PROVERBS 8:12 KJV *"I wisdom dwell with prudence, and find out knowledge of witty inventions."*
Jesus has been made unto us wisdom (I Cor. 1:30), and this scripture repeats it. "Prudence" is practical wisdom, choosing the best means to an end – that leads to shrewd, practical inventions. Since He is your wisdom, keep alert and listen for Him to give you practical inventions. Don't limit yourself to think, "Oh, someone else is smarter than I am. I wouldn't be able to invent that. No, He will give you witty inventions and as you pursue that – keep an open mind. Someone had the idea of a paper clip, W-D 40, bottled water…the list goes on and on. Someone will think of new ways of doing things. It might as well be you!!!! There are discoveries, new inventions, etc. that are waiting to be revealed. Someone needs to think out-of-the-box and discover them – and it might as well be you! George Washington Carver was a Christian man who went to his lab, prayed and listened to hear God instruct him for many products from the peanut. You + God are a majority and He wants to give you wise counsel. Keep an open mind to doing things differently; stay fresh in your approach to situations. ♡♥♡

OCTOBER

10-1

ISAIAH 59:1 KJV *"Behold, the Lord's <u>hand</u> is not shortened, that it cannot save; neither his ear heavy, that it cannot <u>hear</u>."*
"The Lord's hand" is the one and only time this term is recorded in scripture. God's arm is listed several times, but "hand" is unique. It's amazing at times how the touch of someone's hand can encourage and strengthen you. I always want to be under God's hand – it's far better than the good hands of Allstate insurance! His hearing is so good, we can just whisper His Name and we have His attention. What an Awesome God we serve! ♡♥♡

10-2

II TIMOTHY 1:12B KJV *"...nevertheless I am not ashamed: for I know whom I have believed, and am persuaded that He is able to keep that which I have committed unto Him against that day."*
This is one of my favorite scriptures for assurance that God has everything under control. "I know" is very powerful – not "I think," "maybe," "I hope," etc. These phrases are weak, but "I know" is definite and leaves no room for doubt. When you know God's got this – when you let Him have it, you let Him work out the details, you release that situation into His hands, you are fully persuaded and you don't have to worry about it anymore. Whatever you are wrestling with – just give it over to Him and watch Him take care of the situation a lot better than you can ever imagine. ♡♥♡

10-3

PSALM 138:8 NKJV *"The Lord will perfect that which concerns me...."*

This scripture has been a favorite since the years Ted and I were believing God to have children. <u>Anything</u> that concerns you – God has a plan to fix it. *F. J. Dake's comment on "concerns" – "Whatever is necessary beyond keeping me alive in trouble and preserving me from enemies the Lord will do it for me." David was writing this as he was being hunted down by King Saul and his life was on the line. Your life may not be in grave danger, but all of us have "concerns"-- big ones and small ones. You can know that HE will prefect - bring to maturity, fix, correct anything that concerns you. Always know that God is for you – not against you. He loves you!!! ♡♥♡

10-4

ROMANS 5:1 MSG. *"By entering through faith into what God has always wanted to do for us – set us right with Him, make us fit for Him – we have it all together with God because of our Master Jesus."*

Sometimes we look at people whom we think "have it all together." Their lives seem to be perfect. The truth is, without Jesus as the center of your life, you will never have it all together. Our future is bright as we trust Him to guide us into His plans. This takes faith – trust in Him and His Word to guide us, believing He sees the whole picture and every detail that we may not see. Remember, the trust issue must be settled in order to see His plan unfold in your life. As a blood-bought child of God – you indeed have it "all together" in Him! ♡♥♡

10-5

PROVERBS 8:14 NKJV *"Counsel is mine, and sound wisdom; I am understanding, I have strength."*

We really do have everything when we have Jesus as the Lord of our lives. The Word contains not only Who God is for us, but it includes who we are in Him (especially in the epistles; underline the phrases "in him," "in whom," "by whom," etc.). We usually look at Proverbs to share God's wisdom to us. Solomon writes here that God is our counselor, HE gives sound wisdom and understanding and that in itself will give you strength. God is for you – HE wants to equip you to succeed in every area of your life. ♡♥♡

10-6

DEUTERONOMY 6:5 NASV *"You shall love the Lord your God with all your heart, all your soul, and with all your might."*

This entire chapter is rich in study. The instruction the Lord gives is to basically give HIM first place in your heart – spirit, the new birth experience; your soul – your mind, will and emotions; and with all your strength/might – your entire being. God gave specific directions what to do with this instruction in the following verses. Take a look at them. This was not instruction for debate; God wants every part of us. If we keep HIM as the love of our lives, everything else will fall in place. ♡♥♡

10-7

DEUTERONOMY 7:9 NKJV *"Therefore know that the Lord your God, He is God, the faithful God who keeps covenant and mercy for a thousand generations with those who love Him and keep His commandments."*

This is a continuation from yesterday, only in the next chapter. God wrote this for us to KNOW that He is the Lord your God. Again, if we put HIM first place and "love and keep His commandments," He promises to be faithful to us…even to a thousand generations. That's a L-O-N-G time He wants you to KNOW that HE IS the Lord your God. It should be so established in your heart that nothing could ever make you doubt it. (Continued on the next page)

(Continued from previous page)
You <u>know</u> it. You don't need to think if there is some other God
besides Him! He settled it – He is God, and He is the faithful God –
you can count on Him to keep His promises! ♡♥♡

10-8

JEREMIAH 20:11 NKJV *"But the Lord is with me as a mighty,
awesome One. Therefore my persecutors will stumble, and will not
prevail. They will be greatly ashamed, for they will not prosper. Their
everlasting confusion will never be forgotten."*
We all go through situations where we are being taken advantage of,
being mistreated, or just plain under attack by people or the devil.
You must first acknowledge that God <u>is</u> mighty, He <u>is</u> with you and
He <u>is</u> awesome!!!!! So when the trial or attack comes, know that HE
is on your side – those people bringing opposition in your life will
make mistakes and their plans will ultimately fail in their execution.
God is watching over you and He will bring you out on top. Trust
Him. He is AWESOME!!!! ♡♥♡

10-9

JOEL 2:27 NLT *"Then you will know that I am among <u>my people</u>
Israel, that I am the Lord your God, and there is no other. Never again
will my people be disgraced."*
I'm so glad I am included in "My people." The past few posts have
dealt with knowing God IS God and He loves you. You have to
understand that principle and have that as a foundation to build on.
This promise of always being cared for, having plenty of provisions
and being satisfied is reassuring that God has it all covered. Our part
is to trust Him and praise His name. Outside pressures may try to
shame you, but In Christ, we will never be ashamed!!! ♡♥♡

10-10

JOHN 10:10B KJV *"I Am come that they might have life, and that they might have it more abundantly."*

I thought this verse was appropriate for October 10th (10/10). This is a benchmark in my studies. Jesus doesn't want us to have a good life; HE wants us to have life MORE abundantly. One version says "to the full, till it overflows." When Jesus was on this earth He had quite a large ministry. HE had 12-man staff, one of which was a financial officer. To feed the multitude, one of the disciples inferred they had the money to go get food to feed them, but the remote area was the problem. Jesus was not just a poor preacher! He led by example. He is speaking in this verse to encourage us not to settle for just enough – but to ask for and enjoy the abundance, more than enough to meet your needs and have enough to bless others. ♡♥♡

10-11

I SAMUEL 14:36D KJV *"Then the priests said, "Let us draw near to God."*

*For the next 9 days we will look at the phrases "let us" and/or "draw near."

King Saul has just built his first altar to the Lord. The people were about to go to battle and they were making plans to attack the Philistines – their enemy. Now to apply it to us, we are to stay close to Jesus. In modern terms, we don't use the words "draw near" but we do use "come near" and "come close." Today, make time to "come close" to Jesus and give your time and attention to Him. HE is your Best Friend. Time you spend with Him is never wasted time, for you will take on His character and desires. He will help and strengthen you. He will give you "inside information" that will direct you in the right path. Draw near to Him today. ♡♥♡

10-12

PSALM 73:28 NKJV *"But it is good for me to <u>draw near</u> to God; I have put my trust in the Lord God, that I may declare all Your works."*

It's ALWAYS a good idea to go to God when you have a problem. God IS good and He only has good things in store for you. As you trust Him with EVERYTHING in your life, He will be able to do His perfect will in you and for you. David said he put his trust (confidence) in the Lord so that he could testify, declare, and talk about His good works. When God works in your life, tell someone and let your declaration of His goodness be known to encourage other people to trust Him too. "I have put my trust in the Lord God, that I may declare all Your works." If you don't declare it, who will?? ♡♥♡

10-13

ISAIAH 29:13 AMP *"And the Lord said, 'Forasmuch as this people <u>draw near</u> to Me with their mouth and honor Me with their lips but removed their hearts far from Me, and their fear and reverence for Me are a commandment of men that is learned by repetition [without any thought as to the meaning]."*

God is correcting the Israelites because they were serving Him with talk, but not in their walk. Have you ever done something half-heartedly? You were fulfilling your obligation, but your heart and 100% quality effort weren't in it. You walked away and didn't have the joy of that "good job" feeling. The last sentence reveals that people are the ones who teach that God is mean and cold hard-hearted. That's how the "religious" folk perceive our Loving Heavenly Father God. We are to honor God but He does not want us to be afraid of Him. This is a picture of people who really don't have a relationship with God. They just go through the motions. The Lord wants us to enjoy all the benefits of KNOWING Him personally and enjoying His goodness and His blessings as a constant lifestyle. ♡♥♡

10-14

JEREMIAH 30:21B AMP *"I will cause him to <u>draw near</u>, and he will approach Me...."*

There is a time when the wicked will bow their knees and declare that "Jesus is Lord," but it will be too late for them. People think that they are getting by with their sin and turning their backs on God, but there is a pay day coming. We live in a time that God gives the choice to us. He did not make us robots; He gave us a free will. God doesn't "force" His ways on us. He desires us to choose His ways and love Him because we want to. There is a day coming when those who have not made Jesus Lord of their lives voluntarily WILL acknowledge His Lordship. Romans 14:11 says *"every knee shall bow to Me, and every tongue shall confess to God."* Make your choice now to serve Him with all your heart and live the good life!!! ♡♥♡

10-15

EZEKIEL 9:1 NKJV *"Then He called out in my hearing with loud voice saying,"Let those who have charge over the city <u>draw near</u>, each with a deadly weapon in his hand."*

The book of Ezekiel deals with the wrath of God on His enemies. I'm so glad I'm on God's side and will never experience His anger. Can you imagine how God feels, knowing He gave His supreme sacrifice by sending His Son to die for us and take on our sin – only to be rejected? Judgment Day will be coming when we will all stand before the Lord. Make good choices now, so rewards will await you when you stand before the Lord. ♡♥♡

10-16

JOHN 12:32 KJV *"And I, if I be lifted up from the earth, will <u>draw all</u> men unto me."*

Jesus is talking about His death on the cross. He was crucified and lifted up on the tree and took on the curse for all of us. Since He fulfilled this scripture and was lifted up – HE does draw all men to Him. HE is calling, but are you pulling close, coming along side of Him? Again the word "if" signifies the choice we make to enjoy the benefit. Lift Jesus up and let Him be first place in your life, your decisions and your desires. ♡♥♡

10-17

HEBREWS 7:19 TCNT *"For the Law never brought anything to perfection and on the other hand, we have the introduction of a better hope – which enables us to <u>draw near</u> to God."*

When we make Jesus the Lord of our lives, we join the Family of God. God is your Heavenly Father and HE loves for you to come to Him with whatever you need. Under the Law – priests had to go to God for your behalf. Jesus fulfilled the Law which ushered in a Better Covenant that gives us hope and "causes us to <u>draw near</u> to God" personally. Now it is up to us to take advantage of this "family" benefit. ♡♥♡

10-18

HEBREWS 10:22 KJV *"Let us <u>draw near</u> with a true heart in full assurance of faith having our hearts sprinkled from an evil conscience, and our bodies washed with pure water."*

This is a personal invitation to draw near to our God. When we pray, we don't have to wonder if God hears us. We can come boldly in the Name of Jesus with a true and sincere heart and have full access to all heaven has to offer. Through the blood of Jesus – our sins are forgiven and we can be assured that God does hear us. Again, we have the opportunity to come near to God – are you taking full advantage of it?? ♡♥♡

10-19

JAMES 4:8 KJV *"Draw nigh to God, and he will draw nigh to you...."*

I really like this verse! This is a promise God has guaranteed He will do for you. Anytime you get close (draw near) to God, HE WILL hold you close and be near to you too. This is the last of the "draw nigh/near" scriptures. I wanted to end with this one because it is so simple. Again, you need to realize God is for you! HE always wants to bless you and care for you. We are the ones who limit His access to our lives. When hard times come – and they will – pull up next to Jesus and let HIM carry you, that's what He desires to do. The nearer you draw to Him, the nearer He draws to you. Get close to Jesus; He is waiting on you! ♡♥♡

10-20

EPHESIANS 2:8 NKJV *"For by grace you have been saved through faith, and that not of yourselves; it is the gift of God...."*

Don't you enjoy getting gifts? I certainly do. Paul writes so clearly in the Epistles how Jesus has freely given everyone the gift of salvation. It's nothing that we deserved, worked for, or completed any pre-requisites to achieve. God gives us the faith as well as the grace to receive this gift. When you share the salvation gift with other people, make it simple! Share this scripture. The headlines in newspapers daily report how the world is changing and getting worse – people are hurting and need to know Jesus is the protection they need. Don't be shy! ♡♥♡

10-21

EPHESIANS 4:23, 24 NLT *"Instead, let the Spirit renew your thoughts and attitudes (mind)... Put on your new nature, created to be like God – truly righteous and holy."*

Staying on the lines of yesterday – Once we receive God's gift of salvation, there are things that we are responsible for. One BIG one is to renew your mind by the Word of God.

(Continued on the next page)

(Continued from previous page)
Our old nature doesn't automatically go away – we need to exchange our thoughts for HIS thoughts, our beliefs for His truth, our ways to be His ways. We are constantly "putting on the new man" because there is always more to know in the Kingdom of God. There is no boredom; there is always another level to achieve. Keep pressing in to all God has for you!!! ♡♥♡

10-22

PROVERBS 11:25 NKJV *"The generous soul will be made rich, and he who waters will also be watered himself."*
The very basic principle of sowing and reaping is found throughout God's Word. We need to realize that all our actions and words are "seeds." These "seeds" will grow and produce in our lives – good or bad. Live your life the way you want to receive. Think before you act or speak because it will come back to you at some point. Your actions are never lost! God keeps a detailed accounting system and this verse reminds us that we will reap those things we sow. ♡♥♡

10-23

ZECHARIAH 8:12 KJV *"For the seed shall be prosperous; the vine shall give her fruit, and ground shall give her increase, and the heavens shall give their dew; I will cause the remnant of this people to possess <u>all these things</u>."*
God is speaking to the Jewish people, but we can claim this for us today. We ARE His people, and we are His seed. God desires that we are prosperous in our spirit, soul (mind and emotions) and physical body. We should be God's walking billboards declaring His goodness. The "dew of heaven" mentioned represents the many blessings God continuously rains down on our lives. This enables us to not only be blessed, but to be a blessing to others as well. ♡♥♡

Ella C. Brunt

10-24

ROMANS 8:37 NKJV *"Yet in <u>all these things</u> we are more than conquerors though Him Who loved us."*
Yesterday we saw the phrase "all these things" and I wanted to continue looking at that.
"All" means "all." Yesterday's verse referred to blessings and good things. Today Paul is talking about persecutions, tribulations - definitely oppositions that we don't like to think about. But just like in exercise – without resistance there is no muscle-building. In our Christian walk, resistance will make us stronger. Today's Church in China is proof of this principle. In countries around the world, where there is persecution against Christians, there is strength in those people of God. Paul was an "expert" in this field. He faced all kinds of persecutions, but he wrote to encourage us – we are more than conquerors through Jesus. If you are having some resistance in your life, be encouraged, get your strength from HIM and HE will cause you to overcome. God loves us and HE will always be with us and supply everything we need to get us through. ♡♥♡

10-25

PHILIPPIANS 2:14 NKJV *"Do <u>all things</u> without complaining and disputing."*
As you can see, I'm on a "roll" with the phrase "all things." Today's verse can be applied to our lives to be godly examples to those who are looking at the way we handle things – all things. Life is not always "fair." Things come against us that are not pleasant, BUT GOD will use those things to build Godly character in us as we hold our tongue and refuse to complain. When we consider "all things," we are reminded to not just be happy when life is good, but also to walk through the rough places without complaining. Don't let the rough spots steal your joy. Evangelist Jerry Savelle wrote a book and said, "If the devil can't steal your joy, he can't get your goods." Your attitude will help get you through those tough times by knowing God IS with you and will strengthen you. ♡♥♡

10-26

I CORINTHIANS 13:7 NKJV *"Love...bears <u>all things</u>, believes <u>all things</u>, hopes <u>all things</u>, endures <u>all things</u>."*
The <u>Amplified Bible</u> states, *"Love bears up under anything and everything that comes, is ever ready to believe the best of every person, its hopes are fadeless under all circumstances, and it endures everything [without weakening]."*
God's love that has been "shed abroad in our hearts" gives us the capacity to bear up, hope and endure "all these things." When your love capacity runs out, rely on God's love to get you through and enable you. ♡♥♡

10-27

JOB 5:8, 9 AMP *"As for me, I would seek God and inquire of and require Him, and to God would I commit my cause – Who does <u>great things</u>, and <u>unsearchable</u>, <u>marvelous things</u> without number."*
Job is the oldest book in the Bible. Even Job (who did not have scriptures to study, but knew God on a personal basis) declared his desire to seek God and to live for HIM because of His goodness to do great, limitless, and marvelous things. We don't serve God out of fear, but out of love and honor because HE is so very good. In a world filled with hate and fear – we can live victorious because of God's love and His goodness to give us all things to enjoy! ♡♥♡

10-28

DEUTERONOMY 1:18 AMP *"And I commanded you at that time <u>all the things</u> which you should do."*
This is the fifth book that Moses wrote.
So much of this book is a repeat of God's instructions to the children of Israel. God set up the first court system so the people could get their disputes settled. Moses reassures the Israelites what their duties are and encourages them to walk in the ways of God to achieve the victories that are ahead of them. (Continued on the next page)

(Continued from previous page)

You may be going through some situations and you are not quite sure what to do, but God knows <u>exactly</u> what you need to do and HE will tell you when you need to know. Trust Him and learn to listen to hear His voice – He is speaking, so get your "receivers hooked up" and you will know! ♡♥♡

10-29

LUKE 24:14 NKJV *"And they talked together of <u>all these things</u> which had happened."*

Can you put yourselves as one of the two men walking on the Road to Emmaus the same day Jesus arose from the tomb? Their conversation was consumed with the things Jesus had been doing, but now they were distraught with the crucifixion and seeming end to Jesus' ministry and life. The walk was over seven miles, so I'm sure they had a lot to talk about. So what do your conversations sound like? Do the people you hang around with enjoy talking about the things of God? We are living in a time when Jesus' return is very imminent – people need to know of His return and how to be ready to meet Him!!! ♡♥♡

10-30

JOHN 14:25, 26 NKJV *"<u>These things</u> I have spoken to you while being present with you, But the Helper, the Holy Spirit, whom the Father will send in My name, He will teach you <u>all things</u>, and bring to your remembrance <u>all things</u> that I said to you."*

Jesus is talking to His disciples and assuring them that the Holy Spirit is going to come and help them through difficult situations. I love the phrase that He will "teach us all things" and even help us to remember His instructions. I need the Holy Spirit every day to bring back to my memory the Word and God's instructions. This is a promise we need to receive in order to live the blessed life God has for us to enjoy. ♡♥♡

10-31

ACTS 19:41 NKJV *"And when he had said <u>these things</u>, he dismissed the assembly."*

Some of Paul's companions were taken into custody for their Godly beliefs and outspoken remarks about the idols and idol makers in Ephesus. The clerk commented that the charges were not enough to try Alexander. He then dismissed the meeting and let the crowd of Ephesians and Jews go. I see this as "Divine favor" that we have on our lives. As we serve the Lord in our words and actions, HE will give us favor with God and man! When we are in tight places, His favor will be on us – nothing <u>we</u> have done, but what HE does in, through and for us!!! When the Lord is on your side – what can people do to you? ♡♥♡

NOVEMBER

11-1

MARK 10:21 NLT *"Looking at the man, Jesus felt genuine love for him. 'There is still <u>one thing</u> you haven't done,' He told him. 'Go and sell all your possessions and give the money to the poor, and you will have treasure in heaven. Then come, follow Me'."*

Can you picture this – Jesus is giving this young man an invitation to be part of His evangelistic team! Jesus was not trying to take this man's money – He was letting the man realize how much power his possessions had over him that kept him from ultimately following Jesus. The <u>one thing</u> Jesus wanted the rich young ruler to do was to do was OBEY Him. Jesus even told him what the outcome would be "…and you will have treasure in heaven." How many times has Jesus asked us to say, do, or give something and we debated it without obeying? Be quick to obey and watch the Lord give back to you in such a measure you never dreamed possible. ♡♥♡

11-2

LUKE 20:42 MSG. *"<u>One thing</u> only is essential, and Mary has chosen it – it's the main course, and won't be taken from her."*

Now stop and envision this – Jesus comes to your home and is talking – you have a personal audience with the Creator of the universe. Mary sat near Jesus and was soaking in every word He spoke. Her sister Martha was in the kitchen busily preparing a meal. The prior verse says that Martha was "distracted." When Jesus is speaking – are you listening? Don't let distractions take the time that you should be daily sitting close to Jesus and learning His ways. Don't plan your day - and then see if you have time left over to spend with Jesus. Plan your time with Jesus and make it first priority and then you will see how much you can get accomplished in your day. ♡♥♡

11-3

LUKE 20:3 NKJV *"But He answered and said to them, 'I will ask you one thing, and answer Me'."*
We've looked at "one thing is essential" and "one thing you lack". Today let's look at when the scribes, elders and chief priests confronted Jesus in the temple and asked where He got His authority. Jesus answered a question with a question. Jesus asks us as well, "Do you really believe I AM the Son of God?" If He is, then we are to seek Him and do everything in our power to know Him, obey Him and love Him. ♡♥♡

11-4

2 PETER 3:8 KJV *"But, beloved, be not ignorant of this one thing, that one day is with the Lord as a thousand years, and a thousand years as one day."*
Peter is speaking to Believers. He is admonishing us to be intelligent – which means you need to study and NOT be ignorant of God's Word. As you do, you will see that God created T-I-M-E for us, because HE lives in time-less-ness. HE sees our end from the beginning; HE is Omniscient, Omnipotent and Omnipresent. God knows exactly what you are going through, what you are facing. HE also knows how HE is going to get you through and out of it!!! When you are in HIS hands, you have nothing to worry about. He has your life and His plans are very, very good!!! ♡♥♡

11-5

JOHN 9:25 NKJV *"He (the healed blind man) answered and said, 'Whether He (Jesus) is a sinner or not I do not know. One thing I know: that though I was blind, now I see."*
I like this story of the blind man being healed. The blind man admits that he didn't know how it happened – he just knew he was born blind, but after encountering Jesus – he was totally healed. When we have a Close Encounter with Jesus, HE does marvelous things in our lives we can't explain; all we have to do is receive and enjoy the blessings of God on our lives. (Continued on the next page)

Ella C. Brunt

(Continued from previous page)
You may not have all the answers, but <u>one thing</u> you know is that Jesus is The Christ, The Son of The Living God!! ♡♥♡

11-6

PHILIPPIANS 3:13B NKJV *"…but <u>one thing</u> I do, forgetting those things which are behind and reaching forward to those things which are ahead…."*
Paul is writing to the Philippians and he tells them that he personally does not look backward. The past IS the past. You can't take words back OR change the past. Pastor John Osteen used to say, "You can't unscramble eggs." We must let go of the past and look forward. You never accomplish anything looking in the rear-view mirror. Learn from the past, but you have a bright and promising future to focus on and live out in victory!! ♡♥♡

11-7

PSALMS 27:4 NKJV *"<u>One thing</u> I have desired of the Lord, that will I seek: that I may dwell in the house of the Lord all the days of my life, to behold the beauty of the Lord, and to inquire in His temple."*
David's one desire was to please God, just simply to know Him and please Him. His focus was staying in constant fellowship with the Lord, in conversation, with questions and answers. We have the Holy Spirit residing/dwelling in us. Just like David – take time to "behold" Him. You become what you behold and/or spend your time with. What better "Best Friend" could you have but JESUS? ♡♥♡

11-8

PHILIPPIANS 4:6 MSG. *"Don't fret or worry. Instead of worrying pray. Let petitions and praises shape your worries into prayers, letting God know your concerns."*
I love this translation – we waste too much time worrying about things we have absolutely NO control over. This is the best translation I've found about worry and what to do with it. When you catch yourself worrying and fretting about a situation, STOP and start making it a prayer to God. (Continued on the next page)

119

(Continued from previous page)

HE sees the whole situation and knows exactly how to work it out for us. Let your praise and prayers literally SHAPE those worries into prayers. God ANSWERS prayer! So stop wasting time worrying and make it a praise and prayer time – you will see the results! ♡♥♡

11-9

PHILIPPIANS 4:7 MSG. *"Before you know it, a sense of God's wholeness, everything coming together for good, will come and settle you down. It's wonderful what happens when Christ displaces worry at the center of your life."*

As we continue with thoughts concerning "worry" – this scripture lets us know when we release the worry to God as prayer and praise – HE will "settle you down." Have you ever been told by someone when you are really getting emotional to "Settle Down"? Paul writes to us and lets us know that God Himself desires to work in the situation that you are so worried about, to make everything come together and work out for your good. Get your eyes and attention off the problem and onto Jesus – because HE will work things out for our advantage. ♡♥♡

11-10

I JOHN 2:14C NKJV *"…because you are strong, and the word of God abides in you, and you have overcome the wicked one."*

Paul is writing concerning our spiritual condition. I repeat Paul's admonishment – BE STRONG today! The Word of God has been deposited in you and is growing and increasing. You are a winner, an Overcomer, strong in the Lord and the power of HIS might!!!! You sit in victory! The Word of God indwells you and HE puts you over. It's a done deal – the devil is defeated and you win every time he tries to attack you and get you off course. Be encouraged today – God is leading you as you trust Him!! God's got this! ♡♥♡

Ella C. Brunt

11-11

ECCLESIASTES 3:1 NKJV *"To everything there is a season, a time for every purpose under heaven."*

Sometimes we may THINK God is not answering our prayers. One thing I have learned is that God knows the timing for the things HE has prepared for us. Sometimes HE has to prepare us to receive what HE has prepared for us. Don't get discouraged as you wait for the answer to your prayer. Believe God - that HE is doing the "work" in you and for you. Your Father God loves you and has the times and seasons in His hands for you!! ♡♥♡

11-12

ISAIAH 61:7A NKJV *"Instead of your shame you shall have double honor."*

Life situations happen and "shame" may have tried to put you down and discourage you. God is not in the "shame" business. God is in the business of removing shame, blame and disgrace and not only removing it, but giving you double honor! That's enough to encourage you to hold your head up today!!! ♡♥♡

11-13

PSALM 34:7 NKJV *"The angel of the Lord encamps all around those who fear Him, and delivers them."*

As I studied this verse, the commentaries record "the angel" refers to "the manifestation of God's presence." As we honor Him (the term "fear" means reverence, honor); HIS presence will surround us to protect and deliver us from evil. This world is so crazy and we must daily honor God because HE is such a loving God, and the benefit is to have HIS presence and power constantly delivering us. ♡♥♡

11-14

DANIEL 3:25 NKJV *"Look, he answered, I see four men loose, walking in the midst of the fire; and they are not hurt, and the form if the fourth is like the Son of God."*

Daniel is one of my favorite Old Testament Bible characters. Even though he was held hostage in a foreign land, he would not back off his trust in the True and Living God. As we continue to trust in God and His Word – we too can have the power of God manifested in our lives. You are NEVER alone, God lives IN you to provide, guide and deliver you out of dangers that were meant to hurt you. GOD never leaves us, but is always with us. Always keep in mind that God fights for you. God is FOR you, not AGAINST you. You may feel like you are in a hot furnace – but we have The Fourth Man with us every step of the way!!! ♡♥♡

11-15

ISAIAH 58:2A NKJV *"Yet they seek Me daily, and delight to know My ways...."*

This 58th chapter deals with the fast God desires. God begins by encouraging us to seek Him <u>daily</u> and enjoy learning His ways of doing things. We don't fast to change God's mind about something we are praying for. Fasting will change us to be sensitive to know the things that please God and conform to His Will for us. When you have time, read and study this entire chapter to understand the fast that pleases God. Begin with seeking Him and enjoy learning His way of doing things. We conform to His Ways, rather than manipulating Him to conform to what we want. ♡♥♡

11-16

PROVERBS 8:17 NKJV *"I love those who love me, and those who seek me diligently will find Me."*

God is not playing hide-and-go-seek with us. This is a promise to everyone who loves God (because HE IS GOD) and desires to know Him. He gave us the guide book – The Bible – that reveals to us His character, His ways, His benefits, etc. (Continued on the next page)

(Continued from previous page)
Through prayer (talking to God) and studying His Word – you <u>will</u>
find Him and His love will be so strong in you that absolutely
nothing will be able to separate you from His presence and blessings.
If you seek Him, you will find Him! ♡♥♡

11-17

LAMENTATIONS 3:25 NKJV *"The Lord is good to those who wait for
Him, to the soul who seeks Him."*
Jeremiah is writing about the goodness of God even though he was
experiencing great persecution. It is so vital in these last days that
our lives count for Jesus. The Lord is better than "good." Using the
word "good" to describe God is such an understatement. But as we
seek Him to know what HE wants, it automatically carries His
Blessing. We will be successful if we do His Will. ALWAYS seek
Him first before you start making your own plans! Seek, know, and
do what God wants and you will live in His Blessings. ♡♥♡

11-18

PSALM 46:10 KJV *"Be still and know that I am God...."*
"Be still" means "to put your hands down." When it seems that you
have done everything you know to do in the "natural" (pray, trust
God, ask for wisdom, seek God regarding what HE wants to do), this
scripture says to "take your hands off the situation" and let God
work. Don't waste time by always having your hands in things.
From the very beginning, put the situation in His hands and He will
guide you through every circumstance. Be still, get quiet, turn off the
noise, and wait on Him – then you will truly <u>know</u> – God IS God!
♡♥♡

11-19

LAMENTATIONS 3:40 KJV *"Let us search out and examine our ways, and turn back to the Lord."*

As Believers, we should constantly examine and judge ourselves to make sure our motives and our hearts are right. If we take inventory of ourselves and see where things have crept in and gotten us off course, then we need to make the adjustments and return to the Ways of the Lord. None of us are "immune" from the devil's attacks. Temptations will come - but we can overcome every obstacle with Jesus!

I ask you this question if you have stopped trusting in God – How is that working for you? Search out and examine your ways and turn back to the Lord. He HAS everything you need. ♡♥♡

11-20

ACTS 16:31 NKJV *"…Believe on the Lord Jesus Christ, and you will be saved, you and your household."*

The Philippian jailer asked Paul, "What must I do to be saved?" Jesus made salvation so easy for us to receive. If we have unsaved family members then claim this promise that we would be saved AND our household!!! Let your life be an example of Jesus' peace, provision, and health to your family. You don't have to preach to them all the time, but let your life be a godly example and the Lord will do His part to make sure they will have the opportunity to give their lives to Jesus. ♡♥♡

11-21

PSALM 138:2C NKJV *"...for You have magnified Your Word above all Your Name."*

God created everything by speaking it into existence. God holds the world together by the Word of His power (Hebrews 1:3). God gave Jesus the Name that is above all names (Philippians 2:9). But HE has given us HIS WORD – the Bible – to be first place in our lives!!! Make His Word the standard for your living, loving and giving. ♡♥♡

11-22

LUKE 6:36 NKJV *"Therefore be merciful, just as your Father also is merciful."*

Luke was writing about Jesus' teaching on how we are to treat our enemies – those who had mistreated us in some way. Our Father God is so full of mercy. HE has shown us His mercy, no doubt about it. God desires that we be merciful -- full of mercy – to others. This is much easier said than done. As you sow seeds of mercy toward others, you will reap mercy when you need it. Don't try to get even. Show mercy, God's mercy, and see how things will change for His glory. ♡♥♡

11-23

PSALM 37: 34A NKJV *"Wait on the Lord, and keep His way, and He shall exalt you to inherit the land."*

There are so many blessings the Lord wants to give us, but they are not automatic. There is a "waiting on the Lord" that brings those blessings to us. As we spend time with Him in prayer and reading His Word, this is the waiting time. As we give ourselves to obey and keep His ways, this is the preparation time. HE will prepare us to receive His blessings during these times of preparation. Then, He is able to take us into places of blessing. He will enable you to be in control of your sphere of influence. ♡♥♡

11-24

I THESSALONIANS 5:18 KJV *"In everything give thanks: for this is the will of God in Christ Jesus concerning you."*

(As we begin this Thanksgiving week – be full of thanks!)
I like how Paul wrote "IN" everything and not "FOR" everything. We may find ourselves in very uncomfortable situations, but we can always thank God IN those situations and believe HIM to bring us through them. If you ever want to know the will of God – here it is – give thanks IN everything!!!!! ♡♥♡

11-25

COLOSSIANS 1:3 KJV *"We give thanks to God and the Father of our Lord Jesus Christ, praying always for you."*

It is really hard to pray for someone and hold a grudge against them. The Word says to even pray for your enemies! Now that is not easy to do. As we give thanks to God and keep a grateful heart for all HE has done for us, we are enabled to pray for others. Just think, some people have no one praying for them. We can make a difference in someone's life by being the one who will pray for them. On purpose, take a portion of your prayer time to ask God who HE needs you to pray for. Only eternity will tell what He can accomplish in someone else's life through your prayers!!! ♡♥♡

11-26

PSALM 118:29 & 136:1 NKJV *"O give thanks unto the Lord; for he is good! For his mercy endures forever."*

Twice David wrote the exact some words and several other times something similar. Praise and thanksgiving should be such a BIG part of Christians' lives. It should be so automatic to have a thankful heart. Our Lord is "gooder-than-good." Thank God for His mercies that are limitless --and they will last forever! It should be a l-o-n-g list and endless list of things we are thankful for. Just consider all the Lord has done for us. Be thankful! ♡♥♡

11-27

EPHESIANS 5:20 NKJV *"...giving thanks always for all things to God the Father in the name of our Lord Jesus Christ."*

Paul was instructing the church at Ephesus to be thankful – full of thanksgiving -- to the Lord. As Christians, a heart of thanksgiving should be our "normal" mode of operation. Thanksgiving is a season we celebrate in America. Enjoy your friends and family and be a blessing and encouragement today! ♡♥♡

11-28

PSALM 37:23 NKJV *"The steps of a good man are ordered by the Lord, and He delights in his way."*

If you really love someone, you desire to please them and make sure their needs are met. Have you ever thought about loving Jesus so much that you want to please Him and make sure <u>His</u> needs are met? We've read this scripture in the sense we are the "good man" and how our steps are ordered and directed by Him. But look at the second part – "He delights in his way." WHEN we allow Jesus to order our steps/life, HE is pleased with us. The Lord actually delights in us! More than anything in this world – live your life to where Jesus is pleased with you!!♡♥♡

11-29

MALACHI 3:6A NKJV *"For I am the Lord, I do not change."*

We should be appreciative that Our God is the same – HE never changes. This phrase lets us know how very much we can count on His Word. He will do exactly what He said! HE is the "I AM." HE has the capacity to be/do whatever you need. ♡♥♡

11-30

LUKE 15:31 NKJV *"And he said unto him, 'Son, you are always with me, and all that I have is yours.'"*

We are sons and daughters of God. Our Father God is not stingy! HE wants to bless us. The only thing HE desires us to do is to ASK Him.

Many things in our Christian journey are not "automatic." We have access to all God has and is. All of this is already ours, but our responsibility is to ask and receive from Him. Take advantage of everything God has given you – read His Word to be informed of what those blessings are and then ask for them in faith. Believe and receive! ♡♥♡

DECEMBER

12-1

EXODUS 14:14 NKJV *"The Lord shall fight for you, and you shall hold your peace."*

We need to remind ourselves that God really can "do this" all by Himself. HE really doesn't need our input. The Israelites were facing impossible situations, but God reassured them that HE would fight for them and they needed to hold back on their conversations and speech. You may be facing a situation that looks difficult for you. Step back and claim this scripture and remind God that He will fight for you so you don't have to do or say anything. HE is faithful to defend you!!! ♡♥♡

12-2

ROMANS 2:11 KJV *"For there is no respect of persons with God."*

Even though you may think you are God's "favorite child"... we ALL ARE!!!

HE loves us all without partiality. There is nothing you can do for Him in order for Him to love you more or love you less. It is why He is supernatural and we are not. Our humanity cannot understand this concept, but His Word says it, so we can believe it, even if we have to believe it by faith. Rest in His love and care for you. You are in GREAT hands!!! ♡♥♡

12-3

JOHN 15:17 KJV *"These things I <u>command</u> you, that ye love one another."*

Jesus didn't say this as a "suggestion" to think about. This is a "command" that is not an option. When you allow the love of God to rule your emotions, actions, and speech, you are able to love with God's (agape) love which is limitless. ♡♥♡

12-4

HEBREWS 10:35 KJV *"Cast not away therefore your confidence, which hath great recompense of reward."*

Look at this verse in two other versions:

"You must never give up your confident courage" – Williams translation.

"...for it has a great reward awaiting it" – Twentieth Century New Testament.

As long as you are still breathing, you have hope! It's not over yet. Keep your trust/confidence in the Lord and He will bring you out on top. ♡♥♡

12-5

I CORINTHIANS 14:33A KJV *"For God is not the author of confusion, but of peace...."*

Many times when we are faced with decisions, there may be a nervousness or lack of peace. Allow HIS peace to be your guide. God is not in that sense of confusion and indecision. If you don't have peace about something, just wait and don't proceed. It is better to not make a mistake than to try to undo a mistake. ♡♥♡

12-6

I CHRONICLES 16:8 KJV *"Give thanks unto the Lord, call upon His name, make known his deeds among the people."*

Three things David wrote in his first psalm of thanks.

1 - Thank the Lord is the first priority;

2 - Call on His name. When you pray, come in the Name of Jesus and make your requests to the Father;

3 – Testify! Tell others how good God is!! ♡♥♡

12-7

PSALM 66:8 KJV *"O bless our God, ye people, and make the voice of his praise to be heard."*

There is no such thing as "silent praise." The Psalmist encourages the people to bless the Lord, and give honor and thanks to Him. We can go to the sports events and yell and cheer and "praise" our favorite teams, so why should we give God anything less under the guise of being "reverent"? We need to let our praise be heard!!!! Get loud!! ♡♥♡

12-8

PROVERBS 8:14 KJV *"Counsel is mine, and sound wisdom: I am understanding; I have strength."*

As Believers, we are never alone. We have God's abilities living in us, so this is a scripture I claim in prayer, acknowledging that HE is in me and I am in Him. I have His counsel. I have His sound wisdom and understanding. I have His strength. We all need to rely on God's "Divine Side." ♡♥♡

12-9

ROMANS 13:14 NKJV *"But put on the Lord Jesus Christ, and make no provision for the flesh, to fulfill its lusts."*

As long as we live on this earth – we will have the fleshly issues to deal with. We have the responsibility to exercise our spirits and minds to be stronger than our flesh. The way to accomplish that is to "put on" The Word (Jesus) and make a quality decision to keep His Word first place and final authority for everything you do and say. ♡♥♡

12-10

ROMANS 13:12 NKJV *"The night is far spent, the day is at hand. Therefore let us <u>cast off</u> the works of darkness, and let us <u>put on</u> the armor of light."*

We know that we are living in "the last of the last days," so now is the time to "cast off" anything that does not please God and "put on" Godliness in everything we do, say, and think. In each case, it says that WE are to do this. It is our responsibility. God will not do this for us. We have to take the time to maintain our spiritual condition. ♡♥♡

12-11

PSALM 119:89 NKJV *"Forever, O Lord, <u>Your word</u> is settled in heaven."*

One thing is a "sure thing." God said what He meant and meant what He said in His Word. The Psalmist writes His Word is sure and it is eternal. When you are believing God for something, get a scripture reference for it, pray it back to Him and stand until you receive it! ♡♥♡

12-12

PSALM 73:28 NKJV *"But it is good for me to draw near to God; I have put my trust in the Lord God, that I may declare all Your works."*

Preparation time is never wasted time. The time you spend reading the Word, prayer, meditating on God's goodness is always beneficial. It is good for us to "draw near" to Him. The more you know Him, the more you trust Him and you will talk about His works. ♡♥♡

12-13

*As we get approach Christmas, let's look at some familiar Christmas Story scriptures.

LUKE 1:38 NKJV *"Then Mary said, 'Behold the maidservant of the Lord! Let it be to me according to your word.' And the angel departed from her."*

As we count down to Christmas, let's look at some events that preceded the birth of Jesus. The angel came and talked to Mary to let her know that she was to supernaturally conceive and carry God's Son. Her obedience provided the world with God's greatest gift. She surrendered her will to the Will of the Father. May we all be quick to surrender to His will and reap the benefits of total obedience. You may not always understand it, but when you know God has spoken to you, obey and He will take care of the details. ♡♥♡

12-14

MATTHEW 1:20 NKJV *"But while he thought about these things, behold an angel of the Lord appeared to him in a dream, saying 'Joseph, son of David, do not be afraid to take to you Mary your wife, for that which is conceived in her is of the Holy Spirit."*

We credit Mary with her obedience to listen and obey God's command about giving birth to Jesus, but let's look at Joseph. He is engaged to Mary and finds out she is pregnant. He is contemplating "putting her away" when the angel Gabriel appears. As Mary responded in obedience to God's plan, so did Joseph. Both had to totally trust God for something that had never been done before. What an example to follow. Be quick to obey and trust God in whatever situation you are facing today. ♡♥♡

12-15

MATTHEW 1:21 KJV *"And she shall bring forth a son, and thou shalt call his name Jesus; for he shall save his people from their sins."*
This is the first prophecy written in the New Testament. This is the first of four times the angel Gabriel came to Joseph.
The message instructs Joseph what to name this child: Jesus! In Hebrew, this means "Yahweh saves" and declares that Jesus would come and bring salvation from the pollution, power, guilt, and penalty, of sin. I AM SO GRATEFUL Jesus came and fulfilled His mission to save us!!!!! ♡♥♡

12-16

ISAIAH 7:14B KJV *"Behold, the virgin shall conceive, and bear a Son, and shall call His name Immanuel."*
Hundreds of years before, God spoke through Isaiah that Jesus would be born and gave details concerning this great event. Immanuel is Hebrew for "God with us." God was foretelling the virgin birth as well as His Son dwelling with us. You are never alone. Jesus is always dwelling in you. ♡♥♡

12-17

MICAH 5:2 NKJV *"But you, Bethlehem, Ephrathah, Though you are little among the thousands of Judah, Yet out of you shall come forth to Me The One to be ruler in Israel, Whose goings forth have been from old, from everlasting."*
Here is another prophecy concerning the birth of Jesus. This time, it foretells the place of His birth. The Bible IS the infallible WORD OF GOD. No other book has so many fulfilled prophecies. Settle it – God's Word IS sure and is The Truth! ♡♥♡

12-18

LUKE 2:1 NKJV *"And it came to pass in those days that a decree went out from Caesar Augustus that all the world should be registered."*
Governments like to keep track of their citizens. Even more important than this, is our Heavenly Father keeps track of us!
(Continued on the next page)

(Continued from previous page)
HE knows our thoughts, desires, intentions -- everything about us and still HE loves us without limits. Amazing! Know you are loved today by the Creator of all things. ♡♥♡

12-19

LUKE 2:4 NKJV *"And Joseph also went up from Galilee, out of the city of Nazareth, into Judea, to the city of David, which is called Bethlehem, because he was of the house and lineage of David."*
We see that Joseph's home town was Nazareth. Because of his family genealogy, he was required to go to Bethlehem to report for the census and taxation. We can see how Joseph obeyed the laws of the land to pay his taxes and register with the government as required. We too should pay our taxes and be honest with our finances. We can just mail it, but they had to physically travel to pay in person. Paying required taxes shows godly character for sure. ♡♥♡

12-20

LUKE 2:5 NKJV *"…to be registered with Mary his betrothed wife, who was with child."*
This verse lets us know Joseph followed Gabriel's instructions and fulfilled his contract and married Mary. She is in the last days of her pregnancy. I'm sure the travel was not easy, but they went together to fulfill their obligations to the government. Sometimes we are required to do things that aren't easy to accomplish, but if those things are important to God, they should be important to us! ♡♥♡

12-21

LUKE 2:6 AMP *"And while they were there, the time came for her delivery."*
Delivery day eventually comes. Mary and Joseph made it to Bethlehem, took care of business and the day of Jesus' birth arrived. Can you imagine the activities in heaven as the hour approached to fulfill centuries of prophecies??!!! You may have dreams and plans on the inside of you; keep them in your heart, pray over them and "delivery" day – fulfillment -- will arrive! ♡♥♡

12-22

LUKE 2:7A NKJV *"And she brought forth her firstborn Son, and wrapped Him in swaddling cloths...."*
God sent HIS only Son as a gift for us. His plan was to redeem mankind. Jesus was not born into nobility, but into a common family. Jesus was actually born to die - die for our sins to redeem us back to God forever. These "swaddling cloths" were the same kind of wrapping cloths the Jews used to wrap corpses for burial. Newborn infants were wrapped "mummy style" with just their eyes showing. We can see Jesus was literally born to die – for our sins. Even at Jesus' birth, we see His mission in life to be our sacrifice for sin. Oh, what a Love Story!!!! ♡♥♡

12-23

LUKE 2:9 NKJV *"And behold, an angel of the Lord stood before them (the shepherds), and the glory of the Lord shone around them, and they were greatly afraid."*
Now when God has something to say, many times He used angels to be His messengers. These angels were not fat little angels, they are BIG! God's glory was visible and powerful. The shepherds didn't understand and were in awe of the angel's presence. Just one angel was enough to get their attention. Be sensitive to listen and obey God, whether He chooses to speak by His Word with specific instructions, or whether He sends an angel to deliver a personal and powerful message. ♡♥♡

12-24

LUKE 2:11 KJV *"For unto you is born this day in the city of David, a Saviour, which is Christ the Lord."*

Let's break this verse down some. *"This day"* depicts Jesus' humanity because he had a beginning of His earthly mission. *"City of David"* is named for the birthplace of King David, a forerunner of Jesus who reigned as king/priest. *"Saviour"* is the Greek word *"Soter"* which means Savior, Deliverer, Preserver – God's medium of salvation to men. *"Christ"* -- *"Christos"* in the Greek -- means Anointed or Anointed One. (The name "Jesus" references His humanity – not His deity – as the Son of God. God made Him both Lord and Christ (Acts 2:36). HE is the Lord of all power and is able to save; Jesus is Saviour, Christ, and Lord!

God said Jesus was born *"UNTO YOU."* Jesus came for YOU!!!!! Wow, what a plan!!! You are special to God. ♡♥♡

12-25

MERRY CHRISTMAS & HAPPY BIRTHDAY JESUS!

ISAIAH 9:6A KJV *"For unto us a child is born, unto us a son is given...."*

Isaiah could see the man-child born to both the house of Israel and to the world. The child would be God's offspring and be a great light to the people. A Son, not daughter. It took a Man to fulfill the responsibility of redemption of the race – a Man born of a woman and called the Seed of the woman (Gen.3:14). God so loved us, He GAVE His most precious Son. Take some time today to thank God for His most precious gift to us. MERRY CHRISTMAS!!!! ♡♥♡

12-26

MATTHEW 1:25 KJV *"And knew her not till she had brought forth her firstborn son: and he called his name Jesus."*

We've talked a little about the obedience of Joseph to follow God's instructions concerning the birth of Jesus. This verse further expresses Joseph's humility to refrain from physical intimacy with Mary until the Christ child was born. This is just another insight on the character of Joseph. ♡♥♡

12-27

MATTHEW 2:2 NKJV *"...saying, 'Where is He who has been born King of the Jews? For we have seen His star in the East and have come to worship Him'."*
The wise men had travelled a long time from the East. They were astrologers who had seen the star at his birth, but it is possible their journey took about two years before they arrived in Jerusalem. Jesus was born in Bethlehem and this scripture places the wise astrologers in Jerusalem (5 miles south of Bethlehem). The wise men even quoted Micah 5:2 (Mom's thought for Dec. 17th scripture) to the king when they asked him this question. ♡♥♡

12-28

MATTHEW 2:11 NKJV *"And when they were come into the <u>house</u>, they saw the young child with Mary his mother, and fell down, and worshipped Him. And when they had opened their treasures, they presented gifts to Him: gold, frankincense, and myrrh."*
After talking to the King, the star led the wise men to Nazareth where Joseph, Mary, and Jesus lived (Luke 2:39). The star continued to lead them to their "house"-- not the stable where He was born. Jesus was a child by this time, about 2 years old. (I know this blows holes in the "traditional" Christmas story, but let's always stick with The Word as final authority...not a Christmas carol). These gifts were God's provision to sustain this family as they travelled to safety in Egypt and back again! ♡♥♡

12-29

II CORINTHIANS 9:15 NKJV *"Thanks be to God for His indescribable gift!"*
Words are simply not adequate to express the gift of Jesus to the world. But don't let that stop you from forever expressing your thanks to God. I'm sure you received some special gifts for Christmas, but nothing comes close to the gift of Jesus Himself. Have a thankful heart for God's most precious gift to us. Are you thankful for God's gift to you? (Continued on the next page)

(Continued from previous page)
Just think about God's GIFT of Jesus to us. Words are inadequate to describe God's love as He sent Jesus to earth to become flesh, to be sacrificed, to take our place, and to die for our sin. God's gift is unspeakable because words cannot describe just how majestic and mighty Jesus is. Be thankful!!! ♡♥♡

12-30

REVELATION 22:12 NKJV *"And behold, I am coming quickly, and My reward is with Me, to give to every one according to his work."*
Just as we looked at only a few prophecies concerning the first coming of Jesus to earth, the Word has many prophecies concerning his second coming to earth. Just as the first event really happened, so He will return again. We accumulate "works" here on earth. They will be judged as wood, hay, and stubble; or gold, silver and precious stones. One pile will be burned up, and the other pile is what we will have to show for our lives here. Be ready -- be looking for His return, and live your life with pure motives! That is the basis of how He will reward us. ♡♥♡

12-31

REVELATION 22:20B NKJV *"Surely I am coming quickly. Amen. Even so, come Lord Jesus!"*
As we close this year, look at some of the last words written in our Bibles. Just as so many prophecies have already been fulfilled, this verse lets us know that there will be a second advent; Jesus WILL return to the earth! This doctrine is so very important. We must believe and know HE WILL return and we will rule and reign with Him. This earth journey is very short, so make your life count for Christ; it's the only thing you will take into eternity. HAPPY NEW YEAR of new beginnings, new blessings, and new experiences in Him! ♡♥♡

HAVE A WONDERFUL NEW YEAR!!!!!!

Continue the Journey.....

I trust you have enjoyed starting your days with God's Word. I can't emphasize enough how vitally important it is to use The Word as your guide, instruction, comfort, and wisdom. Being a Child of God is progressive. You never get to a point where you have all knowledge and wisdom – but God does. The time you spend with HIM is never wasted time. I believe these short entries get you started on a life-time of daily devotions that will bring you into a close relationship with your Heavenly Father.

In case you have never accepted Jesus as the Lord of your life, let me guide you in this simple process according to Romans 10:9, 10. Pray this prayer – "Almighty God, I come to You in Jesus Name to receive Jesus as the Lord of my life. I believe in my heart and confess with my mouth that Jesus truly is the Son of the Living God. I believe according to Your Word that Jesus came to earth, lived a sinless life, took my sin, sicknesses and diseases and bore them on the cross in my place. You raised Jesus from the dead with Your mighty power. I repent of my sins and shortcomings and receive Your forgiveness by the precious Blood of Jesus. Now I am your child, and You are my Heavenly Father. Take my life and guide me into Your plan. I pray this in Jesus Name, amen."

Living a Christian life is the greatest adventure you will ever experience! God is alive and well and doing great things on the earth today. As you draw near to Jesus, allow The Word to direct your life. You can trust God to lead you into His Blessings that are rich and He adds no sorrow to them as the scripture declares in Proverbs 10:22.

When you mess up, don't run away from God, run to Him! His grace is always extended to you. You and God are a majority in any situation. Trust Him with everything in your life. God is a GOOD God and He loves you so very much.

Now may the Lord who created the heavens and the earth be real to you all the days of your life. May the blessings of the Lord chase you down and overtake you.

Blessings always,
Momma Ella

Other books by Ella C. Brunt –

God Always Wins – America Star Books, LLLP
  ISBN 1588510689 softcover
  ISBN 9781632498434 hardcover
  www.americastarbooks.com
The book chronicles the events of the tragic sailboat accident that took the life of Ella's six year-old son Cody in 1997.
BUT GOD through a series of miracles brought Cody back to life and restored him with a new brain and new lungs. This is a modern miracle story of God's faithfulness to honor His Word and prayer.

It's a God Thing - Volume 2 – W. Publishing an imprint of Thomas Nelson.
ISBN 978-0-529-10551-6
Ella is a contributing author – chapter 16 "God Always Wins".

These books are available on www.amazon.com and Barnes & Noble – www.BN.com